A Way to Go

RHEA WELLS

SilverWood

Published in 2017 by SilverWood Books

SilverWood Books Ltd
14 Small Street, Bristol, BS1 1DE, United Kingdom
www.silverwoodbooks.co.uk

ISBN 978-1-78132-546-9 (paperback)
ISBN 978-1-78132-547-6 (ebook)

British Library Cataloguing in Publication Data
A CIP catalogue record for this book is available from
the British Library

Page design and typesetting by SilverWood Books
Printed on responsibly sourced paper

RHEA WELLS' pioneering approach to teaching, in a variety of educational settings, led to her being asked by colleagues to 'write it all down and tell us how you do it'. So she did, producing articles for Class Room Magazine, Ashton Scholastic, and the New South Wales Educational Department in Australia. A 'scribbler' since childhood, Rhea succumbed, once again, to the mounting pressure to 'write it all down', this time from her family and friends. *A Way to Go* is effectively her memoir and is the result of this continued authorial encouragement.

Rhea has created and publically performed several narrative poems about the vagaries of human behaviour, touching upon long-distance air-travel with an aged parent and birthday tributes. She has co-produced three whimsical, illustrated, Pam Ayre-esque poetry booklets based on the whacky lives of her three pets; a run-away goose, a misplaced whippet and a hand-me-on dachshund. These poems have been well received at public readings in Australia and over-seas.

Other achievements include a BA Honours Degree, a Graduate Diploma in Education, a Graduate Diploma in Teaching English to Speakers of Other Languages, counselling qualifications and more recently a Diploma in Pet Portraiture from London Art College.

Rhea currently resides in South Australia but has a wee bedsit, in the Scottish Borders, to which she escapes when she can, to think, write, create and have fun. A second work, *For the Love of Dog* now awaits her attention.

To Moira

Prologue

I'd come for a reading. I did that off and on. Not with a particular clairvoyant, just any as I felt the need. Seated opposite her, awaiting pronouncements, my eyes meandered to the symbolic images hanging on the walls; steadfast reminders of the more mysterious realms beyond what we less-evolved types understand. My eyes moved on. Shuttered windows – against the summer heat I'd supposed – and incense-infused, velvet drapes languished across the doorway, comfortably dusty; a ticking grandfather clock stood proudly to attention in the hall beyond. No dust there, I noticed. The thick pile carpet beneath my chair stated quality, though it too could have done with a vacuum.

'Danger! Danger! Will Robinson, you're turning into your mother!' My thoughts flashed a warning. Mind, back at the table, it wasn't the knowing gasp or decidedly quickened movement of her hands revealing the cards that hijacked my attention, but the words.

'How do you feel about being pregnant?'

'I'm not,' I blurted, startled.

'The cards disagree,' she said. 'You're about two weeks gone.'

I looked at her in disbelief. She smiled away my ignorance of the ways of her world. 'Tell you what, on your way home, buy a predictor kit and if I'm wrong I'll reimburse you. But you're going to have a girl and she's going to be a mile-a-minute-motor-mouth – a real force to be reckoned with.'

Dutifully, though still disbelieving, I did as she suggested. I was, indeed, pregnant. Not only did my estimation of clairvoyants go up a notch, I was thrilled. Being pregnant was a venture I truly felt ready for. Besides, nature's agenda can't be thwarted. She wants babies. It seemed I was next on the production line. When I told my boyfriend he was as excited as I was. I'd hoped he would be.

Nine and a half months later, after only five hours of labour, our bundle of joy arrived at ten minutes past midnight on 18 January 1984 to the click of Daddy's camera and the haunting theme music of *Blade Runner* – my favourite film at the time.

My best friend and her sister, who both arrived on the scene shortly after Rebecca did – yep, I had a girl – welcomed the new-comer with all the usual comments: 'Oh, she's gorgeous…' 'Can I hold her…?' 'Aw, look at her little upturned button nose…' 'She's just perfect.'

A new way of life had begun. If a little daunting, it was just what was needed, though it took a couple more years for me to fully appreciate that.

Chapter One

What was Lost and what was Found

Dad, whose budding naval career had been cut short by the demands of family life, finally succumbed, at the age of forty-six, to wanderlust and convinced Mum, a stay-at-home housewife, that emigration was best for our family. My seven-years-older sister and I didn't get a say. Decision made. In September 1967, two months before my thirteenth birthday, we set sail on the *Fairsky*, bound for South Australia.

In retrospect, I'd enjoyed my life 'til then, as there was room, at least outside the house, to be a child in the English countryside, chocolate-box Kent village of High Halstow, near the Isle of Grain, on the Hundred of Hoo Peninsula. It was near here, surrounded by wind-ruffled, greenish-gold wheat fields, in which most of us kids played never-ending games of chase, that a number of the village's 600-strong population congregated one sunny morning at Gravesend railway station to witness the end of an era. Aged four, I held onto my dad's hand to watch one of the last steam trains to run.

'OOOFFF! OOOFFF! OOOFFF!!' An enormous bank of smoke-like steam billowed towards us to be nudged aside by a giant cylinder of gleaming black, green and gold, sliding majestically to a stop. It towered above us – a magnificent specimen.

'Oooh! Aaah! Blimey!' Dad snapped to attention – head erect, shoulders squared, a deferential mark of respect. I learnt, later in life, he'd worked on steam engines as a lad. As for me, I had an epiphany: there was more to life than me, my family, and the village. The engine exhaling languorously before me was evidence of an unknown world beyond the current boundaries. Somehow I sensed I'd be part of it one day. For now I was just a little girl holding onto my dad's hand...but the time would come.

Ten minutes later our distinguished visitor pulled away to wherever retired engines go, and Dad and I walked home to 81 Harrison Drive, a semi-detached council house in the Cornish style. For me, the word 'Cornish' equated with 'Ice cream Wafers' – a luscious slab of rich ice cream sandwiched between two yellow wafers, the ice cream so thick licking it made your tongue tired. So, the way the flecks in the white concrete slabs of our house walls used to sparkle, like ice, suggested a more satisfying, if fanciful notion that I lived in an ice cream house.

There were two council house estates in High Halstow: the Big Houses which were reserved for professional/managerial staff at the BP refinery where my dad worked, and the Little Houses, where we lived, which were reserved for the workers. Folk from the Little Houses visited folk in the Big Houses on invitation only.

In addition to the housing estates, our village boasted a primary school, two shops, a fully functioning forge, an 11th Century Norman-built church and our local pub. On Saturday nights in summer, Dad would send me to The Red Dog for lemonade and crisps – Salt and Vinegar (my favourite), or if they'd run out, Smith's with the little twist of blue, waxed-paper which contained salt.

The primary school I attended was just up the road from Number 81 and over the years I survived the usual traumas: bullying, friends moving away, injuries sustained in the schoolyard – mostly from tripping over when running – I did a lot of that. A sign of things to come, perhaps?

By the end of primary school, the education I'd received culminated in my engineering a source of income for Cadbury's Roses chocolates (my favourites) via creation of the Queen Elizabeth Club. My bedroom was HQ and the thruppence entrance fee entitled members to an all-over body tickle via a mitten used fur-side out. Shortly after this entrepreneurial milestone, I passed my 11 plus and was accepted into the Fort Pitt Medway Technical High School for Girls at Chatham High school which, being several miles from the village, made me feel responsible and very grown up. I was having the time of my life as a Pitt Girl. I loved donning the distinctive Persian-blue uniform with its adorable 1920s-styled, round-brimmed felt hat. Indeed, it was a profound honour and privilege to walk through the school gates every morning.

The school and my dad had imprinted their expectations indelibly on me and, in what was to be my first and last year of attendance, I rose to the challenge by coming top in English and art, second in history and well-placed in everything else, except science. Although I scraped a pass, I came bottom of the science class and was completely mortified. I'd let the side down.

My last memory of Fort Pitt was asking for permission from the Headmistress to enter the tunnels beneath the school as research for my next history project. The tunnels had been used, in the 200 years of the building's existence and its varied incarnations by army, religious, nursing and various other personnel. However, there was no chance of a follow-up as Dad's application for emigration had been approved.

As far as life in Australia was concerned, I assumed it would be more of the same, although, as Dad suggested, I might need to ride a horse to school – very Enid Blyton. This romantic notion however was soon blown to smithereens.

The crossing on the Ten Pound POHM (Prisoner of Her Majesty) cruise liner got us off to a promising start. It was a real holiday for most, many never having been on board a ship before, let alone out of the country. The meals were regular and plentiful – breakfast, luncheon and an à la carte dinner served at enormous round tables, set for twelve, with silver service no less. We were spoilt for choice and definitely lulled into a false sense of security.

Following five weeks on the ocean, all the POHMs disembarked in Perth and lived in Fremantle for two days. I felt my parents' uncertainty at the accommodation we'd been provided, following the luxury of cruise ship standards. The rows of camp beds and communal shower blocks with little or no air conditioning was jaw-droppingly basic compared to our floating home. However, the food was reasonable – baked beans, eggs and sausages for breakfast, just like Dad did on Sundays.

In addition, although I'm unsure what my parents had been led to expect, something felt a little off. Instead of being made to feel welcome, our treatment hinted, at times, of disrespect, disdain, even pity. We'd somehow lost status, as if we were refugees rather than legitimate new arrivals. It was very disconcerting.

From Fremantle, we were herded onto trains and delivered, three days later, tired and disgruntled into Adelaide. The temperature on the train proved stifling, as the windows let more heat in than out. Unaccustomed to such ferocious heat, perspiration – not sweat, we were English – trickled relentlessly from our foreheads.

Nor could one avoid body odours, sweaty socks or bad breath – one's own or others – as there'd only been the train's tiny, grimy, stainless-steel basins in toilet cubicles which stank of urine to freshen up in. Though you could try your luck in the mad dash for the loos – which also stank of urine – whenever the train stopped at a station.

As well, because there were no sleeping berths, we'd slept sitting upright. Many of the children slept on the floor in makeshift beds with coats as blankets and bundled-up clothes for pillows. My family members were definitely out of their comfort zone.

The last leg of our journey was a ten-hour bus trip to Whyalla, a hot and windy, dusty-red, iron ore town where Dad had been promised a position at a refinery. The weeks of anticipation and excitement were over.

Three hundred and eighty kilometres from Adelaide's General Post Office and a very, very long way from the home we'd left behind, we stood outside our new one at 4 Mebberson Street. Surrounded by a square of red dust the house sat subdued, contained by a glinting taut wire fence, waiting, as we were, for what would happen next.

'Right,' said Dad. 'Where are the keys?'

'Here,' said Mum. 'Permit me.'

She slid the key in the lock and opened the door. As soon as she did a blast of hot air rushed to greet us; it was as if the house had been holding its breath.

'Phwar!' exclaimed Mum. 'We'll need to do something about this heat, Fred.'

Nothing could have prepared us for the life we were now forced to embrace. It was mostly the little things – it often is – although in Dad's case it was also a big one. The refinery he'd been promised a job at hadn't yet been built. Sure, we'd been assigned a house, but he felt completely duped. He'd uprooted his family to make a new life, a better life, for all. Instead, he was facing unemployment. This was not okay. He approached Broken Hill Proprietors (BHP) steelworks in Whyalla. They were willing to 'give him a go' as long as he obtained his boiler room ticket. Dad was sorted. But not so the rest of us.

As my sister, then almost twenty, had completed beautician training with Yardley of London, she managed to score a job at the local pharmacy. This was a bit of a come down from assisting the rich and famous or hair modelling for Vidal Sassoon, but we were now living in an Australian working man's town. No need to look glamorous out here. This was Whyalla, not catwalk country. Before long she met the young man she would later marry. So she was sorted. That left Mum and me.

Mum hadn't said much since our arrival. Towards the end of the third month her frustration and disillusionment squirmed its way out. She'd had it. No matter how hard she tried, she couldn't combat the film of red dust, which settled on everything. No amount of dusting, washing or wiping helped. Nor did it help that our backyard wasn't green and lush and full of fruit trees and vegetables, like it was in the United Kingdom. Instead, we had a two foot deep dust bowl, which turned to mud the minute any moisture turned up (courtesy of Dad's many futile garden-creation schemes).

That South Australia is renowned for being the driest state in Australia was another of Mum's issues. She couldn't stand the heat. Lying around, sweating profusely and unable to keep the house clean was difficult for a house-proud woman. Then there was me. Almost thirteen with no life experience, other than twelve relatively sheltered years in England, everything was alien. Disappointingly, there was no horse to take me to school, just a clapped-out bus, driven by a maniac who took great delight in taking every curve at tyre-screeching speed, terrorising me if no one else.

Nor were there any lush green fields to run around in, only brand spanking new, bitumen roads that looked like giant flattened liquorice snakes – black and menacing. And, although we'd arrived in spring, it was already reaching 30 degrees Celsius. It was too hot to leave the house for long. My fair English skin burnt as soon as the sun caught sight of it.

School didn't help matters either. No smart uniforms or clear behavioural guidelines there. Everyone, students and teachers alike, were yelling in class. This was unheard of, and I was stunned and concerned. I couldn't hear or concentrate on what the teachers were saying and became increasingly anxious. I liked learning; it was fun or had been. Overwhelmed and frustrated to the point of tears everyday, I simply didn't get it and due to the tears the other kids didn't get me.

'What's wrong with the new kid, Sir?'

Lonely, sad and friendless, I lost my appetite and became withdrawn. To make matters worse, there was talk of my repeating first year if I didn't pass the end of year exams, which were two months away. Determined not to be held back I put my mind to it, passed all my exams and suffered an attack of hysterics from the effort.

Mum, concerned for my emotional well-being, as well as her own probably, had words with Dad (and possibly some higher power) about moving elsewhere. Someone was obviously listening because soon after my emotional outburst Dad spotted the word 'oil' on a piece of newspaper in the rubbish bin. Curious, he pulled it out and read that jobs were available at an oil refinery further south. He applied and was offered a position 380 kilometres away. So, four months after our arrival in Whyalla, Mum, Dad and I moved again. My sister, newly engaged, was determined to stay put. Dad, for some reason, didn't object.

Big changes for everyone, but this time life was smiling as Christies Beach was a properly established coastal town and only twenty minutes' car drive from Adelaide city. Heaven! Mum, Dad and I settled in for the duration.

Chapter Two

Defining Roles and Spiritual Dimensions

By the time I turned seventeen, bouncing breasts had come into their own and I discovered boys. My centre of balance was no longer clear (in more ways than one) and I failed fourth year. Shocked and humiliated, I begged my parents to let me repeat. They agreed but Dad, ever determined to secure my success in life, insisted I complete a one-year secretarial course as well.

Two years later, and still hopeful of going to university, I returned to school as a nineteen-year-old, mature-age student. An 'A' for English that year placed me in the top five per cent of the State, securing my place at university. I was completely stoked, as the Aussies say.

At this point Mum and Dad announced they didn't have the funds to support me further so I applied for a government Tertiary Education Assistance Scheme (TEAS) allowance. To qualify I had to prove financial independence. This required living away from home and supporting myself for a minimum of two years.

Buxom and sporting teeth braces (another of Dad's well-meant interventions) I joined a performing arts centre and sat the public service entrance exams. In the process I gained a boyfriend and employment as a typist. Whoo hoo! Personal freedom away from my parents' well-meaning but often suppressive influence beckoned.

Flush with funds – a whopping $103 a week – I, a short, shy, prim, plumpish, blonde, Bridget Jones type, moved into a share house with two tall, good-looking, blonde-haired demigods (one of whom was my boyfriend) and two tall, tanned, terrific, slim, trim

Abba look-a-like sisters. And although I was not up to much in bed (though I got that sorted out eventually) I liked baking and was a good bet with my share of the rent, so I was in.

I'd begun taking professional voice lessons, so I auditioned for evening work as an entertainer in a restaurant. I was soon ushered out by a staff member who whispered in my ear, 'The boss is not serious about hiring you. He just wants to grope your tits.'

Undeterred, I auditioned for a small role in a semi-professional musical company. The girl ahead of me got the part. She'd been decidedly off-key but was the musical director's lover. I began to lose interest in the theatrical world; it was too superficial for my taste. So I stopped taking singing lessons. That decision ended any potential as a professional singer. But I didn't mind as I was working my way towards attending university. If I succeeded I'd be the first one in the entire history of our family to do so. That would make my parents proud and possibly provide a greater purpose for my life.

In the meantime, there was lots to occupy my mind, such as the constant parties and turn over of housemates, which ensured I'd experiment with all known social drugs available at the time. First cab off the rank was laughing gas. Someone knew someone whose father was a dentist – you know how it goes – and very soon a tank of the stuff turned up. One balloonful and I not only sounded like Donald Duck but I was floating in deep, inky space attached to Earth via a gleaming silver cord extending from my navel.

'Boy, Earth's a long way away,' I mused, when TWANG, the cord pulled taut and I was instantly back in the room. When I regained normal functioning I asked a fellow gas guzzler if they knew what happened if the cord snapped.

'You'd probably die,' he said.

Not long after that, a fiancée of one of our housemates did – in a car crash. I was doing my best to support him in his grief when he responded aggressively to something I'd said. Surprised at his unexpected rudeness I playfully slapped his face and received a well-placed punch in the mouth. I guess that's one way to help the grieving process. My boyfriend gallantly announced, 'No one does that to my friends. Come on, Rhea. Let's get out of here.' A few days later we moved out.

In need of additional cash to cover rent we started a window cleaning service, occasionally incorporating floor polishing as part of the deal. One day we overdid it and turned the floor of a tennis club room into a skating rink. An elderly patron slipped and badly sprained her ankle. Our business limped too after that and then we were bored with it.

Next, I tried waitressing but was sacked on my second night for hitting a drunken patron over the head with my tray when he grabbed my backside. After that I worked for a few months as a kitchen hand in the Green Room at Adelaide's Festival Theatre where I served meals to celebrities. Some were much nicer than others but I've forgotten who was which.

My boobs may have gotten me my next job. Whatever. Being very voluptuous in a tight fitting sweater, saucily short skirt and snakeskin heels was no match for technology. I couldn't operate a PBX 64 switchboard to save my life and overheard the manager ask, 'Who's the idiot that keeps cutting us off?' No surprise that I was sacked after three weeks.

Still chasing dollars, we were forced to move to the cheapest place we could find to stay in.

Our new house had only three walls as the fourth had fallen down and never been rebuilt. On the bright side, it was cheap and an adventure. But it was flipping freezing! Even with nine blankets – yep, nine – I was still cold.

After ten months of alfresco living, I grew polyps in my throat. The doctor said if they got any bigger I'd need to have them scraped off, which would permanently damage my vocal cords.

As I didn't wish to lose my voice, my boyfriend suggested two things: we move back to Adelaide and we commence seeing other people.

'A fresh move, a fresh start,' he said.

His change of heart about the nature of our relationship came out of left field and definitely hurt. I had hoped we would marry in due course, but I didn't ask him about his decision. I was too young and inexperienced to cope with the answer, I guess. We continued to share a house but had separate bedrooms.

Stoically, I got on with my life and got work as a copy typist for *Get Out*, a what's on guide to Adelaide entertainment. Out of seven regular staff, all university students, I was the only paid member, receiving $87 a week. For this I typed from 6.30pm every Monday evening all through the night to meet the magazine's Tuesday lunchtime deadline.

I loved the office locale, it was in Sym Choon's Fireworks Factory, which sounds, far quainter and more exotic than the cheap, rundown place it actually was. Perched precariously at the top of an old rickety staircase in a semi-derelict five-storey building, shafts of dancing dust would waft dreamily in the sunlight that streamed through the cracks – of which there were plenty. Two steps were actually missing near the top of the stairwell and you could see right through the splintered core of the building to the flagstones far below. Insurance? Of course not. Not to worry, it was fun and interesting to work there.

One evening, as the official entertainment reviewer had called in sick, the task fell on my shoulders to attend. I didn't think much of the main act but thoroughly enjoyed the inaugural performance of their support band, *Split Enz*. At another gig, I met Stéphane Grappelli, the world-renowned virtuoso jazz violinist. Accompanying the reporter, I was asked to wait outside the interview suite. When I met Mr Grappelli, he apologised for making me wait and lifted my hand to his lips. 'So suave,' I thought, 'for a bloke whose own hands were insured for a truckload of money.' I was putty. He was gay!

I was also amused to be the only one left in the building the time a tsunami was predicted to hit the coast eight miles away. Don Dunstan, the then South Australian Premier was at the beach. An act of good faith, perhaps? The rest of the *Get Out* staff was heading for the hills, but I just kept on typing.

A year later I was at university full-time and my ex-boyfriend, having found a new love, announced that he would be moving into another place with her. Fair enough, but where would I go? I certainly couldn't afford to cover rent on my own and returning to Mum and Dad's Victorianesque parenting style was not an option.

Forced back into house sharing, I moved in with a trendy couple. That didn't last long. I wasn't trendy enough. The next arrangement was in the home of a bloke with a one legged parrot called Bert and a woman who got plastered nearly every night. Using the cack-brown plastic concertina door to my bedroom as a shield, she would hurl abuse at me and, more often than not, pieces of furniture, though she never once came in. Somehow I was able to continue studying despite her racket.

The next place I stayed in was a room in the home of a young university professor. It was a great arrangement for me although I played havoc on his nerves. At one point he'd temporarily lost his driver's licence, so I'd been ferrying him around. One day I stalled the car on a level crossing just as a train was approaching. Seated in the passenger seat the poor love just about had an apoplectic fit. He turned a strange colour and made some very odd noises. I finally managed to floor it, accelerating away from the oncoming train.

'See. No point in panicking,' I said, affably.

Another night, something woke me from a solid sleep. I lay in the darkness, breathing softly. Then I heard it again, the noise at the window. It was close to my bed.

'Ffft!'

At the same time an eerie, iridescent green glow emanated from outside.

'There's someone out there,' I thought, 'and the window's open.' My heart and mind began to race.

Then, not fifty centimetres from my face, a black leather-gloved hand reached through the open window groping intently for the catch. A stream of defences ran through my mind. What should I do? Call out? Bite the hand hard? Scream? I dismissed all of them.

There was, it seemed, only one recourse, so I took it. Sweat prickling my armpits, heart pounding, face on fire, I burst into view and in a deep voice, which I've never since been able to reproduce, boomed, 'BALLY PEE OFF!'

My surprise appearance must have registered fully as startled eyes stared back in disbelief from behind the balaclava. The ugly red felt mouth-section quivered slightly. The intruder stepped back, straightened, turned and bolted, his feet crunching along the gravelled driveway. I scrambled for the front door, flinging it wide and watched him go, overcoat flapping.

Full of adrenalin, I threw myself on my landlord's bedroom door, hammering hard, 'Wake up! Wake up! We've had a burglar!'

'Oh, Gawd… It's the middle of the night. Ring the police,' came the disgruntled reply.

The boys in blue arrived forty minutes later, by which time my landlord had roused him self sufficiently to take in my story. He was vaguely sympathetic. In fact, I felt sorry for him; woken from a blissful sleep by his exasperating tenant yelling, 'Burglar!' at the top of her voice. Now, here he sat entertaining the local constabulary.

'More tea?'

'No thanks. We've got the details on what appears to be the fourth attempt of this chap we've dubbed the Unley Rapist.'

My jaw dropped.

'We'll be on our way.'

We said our goodnights and after a drink to steady my nerves I returned to my room. Neither my landlord or I wanted a repeat performance, although I suspected his motivation for immediately nailing the window permanently shut may have been to ensure he got a good night sleep, rather than deterring any would-be rapists.

Life carried on. Three years of university later I'd completed my degree. Aged twenty-three, it was time to take stock. Although reasonably good at my studies, academia was really not for me any more than singing was. What to do? I remembered playing 'school' in Dad's old budgie shed in the back garden in High Halstow, so thought teaching might be a good move. I enrolled in a Graduate Diploma. Despite this decision, life remained a little empty.

Still single, unloved by that special someone and disenchanted with Lady Luck, when it came to my love life, I took matters into my own hands and made a move on a young guy I'd met in the university car park. He was definitely not a suitable candidate, but I'd not read the signs and it was another recipe for disaster. I subsequently married and divorced him in quick succession. However, something happened during this time that strengthened my resolve to go it alone in life should this be required of me. I had an OBE; an out-of-body experience.

One afternoon, when my then-fiancé was away for work, I went for a drive with a group of friends. As we set off, I mentioned that I had a feeling we were going to have an accident. It was downplayed, and needing petrol and oil, we drove to a local service station. The petrol paid for, I snuck an oil bottle into the car as we left, not realising the lid was loose. As we turned a sharp corner the oil spilt across the footwell and we were forced to stop and clean up. I was still anxious about my premonition so Aaron, the driver, suggested he drop me home. Thinking I was being silly, I declined the offer.

On the return journey later that night, as we were rounding a curve on the crest of a hill, Aaron, blinded by the lights of an oncoming car, lost his sense of the road. CRUNCH! The tyres on the left hand side hit the shoulder in an escalating rush of gravel and we were viciously catapulted towards the tree that was looming large in our headlights. The next thing I remember was hearing a girl's name being repeated very quietly, as if from a long distance.

'Not my leg. Don't touch my leg,' I stammered before blacking out.

When I opened my eyes I was lying on a trolley in the corridor of a building. A man I didn't recognise was holding my hand.

I passed out once more. This time I was floating in the top-most corner of a dimly lit operating theatre. Below me, with back turned, was a white-coated person ministering to someone lying on a table. That the 'someone' was me finally registered. How odd. There was no need. I was content and at peace (wherever I'd been 'til then) and tried telepathically to tell my attendant to, 'Leave the doll alone.

She's happy and doesn't want to come back.' I then felt something pulling at my face.

Opening my eyes I said to the doctor peering at me, 'What are you doing?'

He replied with a smile, 'Sewing your face back together.'

'Do a good job, won't you?' I said before passing out again.

I had sustained a compound fracture of the right tibia and a badly lacerated head. I believe I survived because I had unfinished business here on the earth plane. I wasn't sure what that unfinished business was, but as I was still here I would no doubt find out.

Newly engaged, recuperating at my mum and dad's, and excited about my vocational posting (teaching graduates were guaranteed employment), I spent recruitment time calling the education department from my sick bed, reminding administration that not to overlook me was, at that point, the most sensible solution.

At the completion of the recruitment period I received a letter stating my application had been unsuccessful and all positions were now filled. I was ropeable and rang the department to advise I'd be coming in to speak, in person, to the employment officer. On crutches, leg in a full cast and accompanied by Mum, who had a really bad cold, we took a taxi, train, then a bus – yep, I am that determined – to the education building. Taking the lift to the appropriate floor I spied the bloke responsible for the oversight sneaking away, or so I thought, along the back of the department. Lifting a crutch, I pointed it towards him and declared, 'Oi, I want to speak to you!'

Any indication of my polite English Rose persona had completely disappeared. He came straight over.

'What seems to be the trouble?'

I told him I wanted the position I was entitled to as a graduate. Forty minutes later I had a job, not seven hundred kilometres from home as I'd expected, but three! See, it's definitely not what you know.

As for my marriage, five months after saying 'I do' I decided, after enduring mental and physical abuse at the hands of a young man who'd promised to love, honour and cherish me, that he definitely didn't, and I left.

So, at the end of my first year of teaching I'd lost my home, my possessions and my husband, but as I no longer believed I'd cheated death to be with him I thought there had to be something else I'd been brought back for.

Chapter Three

Onward, Upward and Beyond

By the end of my second year as a teacher I was living in a nicely appointed flat a million emotional miles away from my disastrous union. Still determined to find my place in the world, I returned to the theatre, as an amateur set designer for a fledgling musical company, and met my baby's daddy.

Several months later, recently divorced, two weeks pregnant and flush with compensation money from the car accident, I bought a house complete with resident ghost. My boyfriend also moved in, but we were too busy expecting to take much notice of apparitions.

About six months after beautiful Reb's arrival, I was awoken by something firmly prodding my collarbone. Disoriented, I sat up, and standing at the side of my bed was an elderly man wearing a blue roll neck jumper and blue trousers. A naval officer, perhaps? I didn't recognise him but he may have been one of Dad's eleven brothers, several of whom had lost their lives in the Second World War. I didn't get a chance to ask as he quickly faded away. I was more intrigued than afraid and went back to sleep.

The following morning, when I spoke to my boyfriend about not sleeping well he commented that he didn't either. As he wasn't one for making a fuss, we simply moved our bed into the sunroom. No more bother – for a while.

The activity in our original bedroom gradually intensified. There were definitely noises that couldn't be heard anywhere else in the house such as water dripping, creaks, groans and tap-tap-tappings. Plus, it was colder than the other rooms. Visitors noticed this too.

I consulted a clairvoyant to find out if there was anything we could do. She recommended exorcism. So, with the assistance of friends, I sprinkled salt round the doorways and window frames, lit two white candles and one of my friends, not me – I felt really idiotic – told whatever it was, politely but firmly, to leave; it was no longer welcome. We then had to wait for the candles to go out. Both candles were identical. One burnt down after twenty minutes. The other was still going after forty. Each time my friend checked to see how far it had burnt it would flare up again. I know, I know, we were giving it more oxygen each time we opened the door – but still!

The third time she checked I lost my cool and snapped, 'For God's sake, leave the door shut and let the bloomin' thing go out!'

After what seemed like an eternity, it did. But it wasn't until Reb began leaning out of her highchair to wave to someone or something I couldn't see, up in the corner of the ceiling, that I began to think, 'I can't cope with this.'

The last straw occurred when I awoke again one night to feel my bedclothes being whipped back from my body, not crossways but downwards, exposing me to the waist. Without looking up to see who or what it was, I grabbed the covers from behind me and yanked them up over my head.

'Get lost,' I growled.

They did. I have not seen any unearthly visitors since, but now and again I sense a presence and wonder if he/they are still around.

Life in Adelaide settled into a routine. My boyfriend worked away, in field catering, leaving me to get on with things. Ever resourceful, I rigged up curtains around the windows of my Volkswagen Beetle. Since breastfeeding in public was not socially acceptable back then, Reb and I spent many happy hours fuelling-up and zipping about in our mobile nursery.

However, after about a year, the humdrum of everyday life began to wear on me and, despite my enjoyment of motherhood and continued involvement with amateur dramatics, the dream of one day living in Sydney (which I'd once visited as a teenager) resurfaced. I told my boyfriend of my desire to relocate and started looking for something affordable in what was rapidly becoming one of the most expensive cities in the world.

Three weeks after an initial enquiry, a Sydney-based estate agent called me back and said, 'If you're serious about purchasing the terraced property, you'll need to get here pronto and check it out.'

So on the day my latest theatrical performance was to be videoed, having first assured the director, 'Of course I'll be back in time,' I rose at 4am, puttered along in dawn light to Adelaide airport, boarded an early morning flight and took off for realms unknown, two states away.

Arriving in Sydney around 9am, I took a taxi to Glebe, ate breakfast at one of the many eateries on Glebe Point Road and familiarised myself with the area: a densely populated, up-and-coming Sydney suburb two kilometres from Darling Harbour and not so far from the world famous Sydney Opera House.

Around 11am I met the agent for a guided tour of the terrace. He had said on the phone that the place was as cheap as chips. I now asked why.

'It's a deceased estate. No one's lived here for over two years.'

Ah!

The interior was exceedingly dark and dank. Tentatively I poked one of the walls with my finger, once my eyes had adjusted to the lack of light. A sizeable chunk of plaster dropped to the floor. That wasn't good.

Undeterred I continued my inspection. The right side wall was missing from the small covered walkway between the original two-up, two-down dwelling and the kitchen. From the look of things the missing wall had served as the back entrance.

Minimalistically kitted-out, a small section of slanting workbench hung on one wall and a tiny stained sink was squished, sulking in a corner. There was, at least, a stove in the kitchen but I was informed it didn't work. It hadn't really looked like it would. Hmmm. I headed outside, watching where I put my feet. The floorboards were loose.

The backyard was concrete, there was no greenery, although

a small tree next door hung limply over the fence providing a hint of shade midway along. Tucked into the far corner was a free-standing concrete cubicle – the toilet. Not only was it filthy, it flushed noisily. The falling down structure that I thought was a shed turned out to be the bathroom. Not much more than a lean-to it, like the toilet, could only be accessed by walking outside. The bath rested on bricks. Interesting. I checked the taps. They worked.

I went upstairs listening for creaks and groans – the stairs, not mine – there weren't any, and I liked the feel of the smooth, wooden handrail; it was warm and somehow comforting.

Upstairs fared better. A double set of French doors in the front bedroom opened onto a balcony overlooking the street. 'A nice place to have breakfast,' I mused. Thankfully the balcony was sound, there was no evidence of rotting timbers or rusty wrought iron and the French doors shut properly.

The two fireplaces, one in each of the bedrooms, appeared to be in good order although they would need to be checked. And the floorboards, despite being covered in five layers of lino were, when I finally found them, pretty solid-looking. I bounced up and down on the floors in both bedrooms to make sure. The only spongy bit was a small patch on the stair landing, but this wasn't a major concern.

I wasn't there long, but I'd made up my mind. The dream of 'living the dream' had won.

'I'll take it,' I said.

Returning to Sydney Airport for 2pm, I flew back to Adelaide, drove to the theatre, ate a light meal and got into costume raring to go for the 8pm curtain. If I tried to do that today I'd never make it.

Further guaranteeing the frenzied whirl of activity unleashed by my decision, our home was put on the market a couple of weeks later. It sold the very next day.

I applied for a year's leave without pay from my teaching position, filled a one tonne truck to capacity and with Reb, then 15 months old, Nanoo the dog, and a couple of acquaintances who also yearned for a more cosmopolitan lifestyle than Adelaide offered, set off in a two vehicle convoy. My boyfriend joined us later when his job wound up.

What a trip! I knew it was a long way – about 1600 kilometres – but hadn't factored in the heat, plus there was no air conditioning. Reb became fitful. Each time she grizzled, Nanoo did too out of canine loyalty.

By the end of the first day, after almost ten hours on the road, discounting loo and coffee breaks, I developed a bit of a headache. It was time to stop for the night. Unsure of how far we'd get on the first leg, I hadn't rung any caravan parks. Those we now tried were booked out. By 9pm we gave up – most of the parks were not dog-friendly anyway – and pulled onto a grassy verge.

Not long after, it started raining. It wasn't a light friendly drizzle, but a stream of heavy raindrops that didn't let up. While my associates grappled with the dynamics of how best to sleep in a sedan, I had my own set of organisational requirements to reach. I decided that Reb and Nanoo would be best snuggled-up, safely locked in the cab of the truck. I then struggled into a sleeping bag, sandwiched between the ground and the bottom of the one-tonner; it wasn't a lot of space but at least I was out of the rain.

The second day of travel I rang ahead and booked a spot in a caravan park for the night. Arriving early in the evening, hot and sticky, we all opted for a shower. My travelling companions, both male, were in a different shower block to Reb and me. Reb slept soundly in her pusher outside the shower door, which I kept open with a rolled-up towel. Nanoo stayed in the truck – on guard.

I forgot to mention that at the time I was undergoing treatment which required the insertion of a nightly pessary, and way past tired, I'd not realised I'd been pushing the diamond-shaped medicant where it was not designed to go.

'Why…won't…it…go…in? I mumbled to myself, struggling.

Suddenly something gave and my you-know-what felt like it was on fire. That wasn't right.

'Help!' I called out, legs crossed, keeling over.

It's really difficult trying to yell for help without waking your child.

'HELP!' I bawled, risking it.

A park attendant heard me. 'What's up?' he enquired from outside the shower block.

'I don't know but I'm in agony.'

Alarmed, the attendant told me to hang on while he ran to the office for assistance. I got dressed, still on fire, and put the still sleeping Reb in the cab of the van.

The park's night manager then gave me directions for the local hospital and off we went – Reb, Nanoo, one of my friends, the truck, me 'n' all.

When we got to the hospital the duty nurse informed me that she thought I'd pushed the pessary into my urinary rather than my vaginal tract. That would explain why it had felt so tight, plus the burning feeling – like a concentrated dose of cystitis. She expressed amazement that I'd managed it. 'You must've been very relaxed,' she said.

I wasn't relaxed now!

She recommended I drink something to make me urinate. I chose beer, bought from an all-night bottle-o, and back at the park downed as much as I could, which wasn't much – I've never been much of a drinker – before falling asleep again under the truck.

By daybreak, I felt a lot better and off we went once more. Halfway through our third day on the road, we stopped for the last petrol fill before finally reaching our destination. A chap asked me where I was heading.

'Sydney,' I announced, brightly.

'I'll give you three years,' he said. 'Three years and I'll bet you'll wanna get out.'

'Okay,' I said, not believing him. He was right.

Chapter Four

Life in the Big Smoke

Initially entranced by my newfound status as a Sydneysider, as predicted, it didn't take long for the gloss to wear off. Sure, I wasn't far from a street lined with trendy eating establishments and several of the world's leading landmarks, but I'd bought a 100-year-old deceased estate. I was now paying for the privilege of living in a termite, flea, cockroach and mouse-infested dump with salt damp, no hot running water, heating or adequate ventilation, hardly any natural light, and an outside loo. But the staircase handrail was beautiful and estimated by the architect to be circa 1898. The four-and-a-half year trial had begun.

There was a bit to do to make the place into a proper home. I had to remove an internal wall, rebuild the kitchen and bathroom, and paint and decorate right through. Was I fazed that apart from some minor renovations I'd never tackled anything quite like this? That I'd likely be doing the majority of the work unassisted? That I didn't have an income? That I had a toddler and pet pooch on my hands? Nope. I like a challenge.

When my boyfriend arrived a couple of weeks later, he agreed to be a stay-at-home hands-on dad 'til I found some contract teaching work, which I did within a couple of days. He then remained at home for several months before announcing he not only wanted gainful employment, he needed a bigger life; sounded fair to me. He applied for and obtained a kitchen hand position in a wine bar on the corner of our street. Perfect.

Since Reb was now old enough to be placed into childcare,

I'd accepted a permanent posting at a college. On her first morning at the kindie (kindergarten), I'd expected tears and a bit of a tantrum. Instead with a cheery little wave of her hand, while I stood blowing my nose at the entrance, she called out, 'Bye, Mum,' over her shoulder, and disappeared into the building.

We then agreed, since my boyfriend kept very late hours, that it would be better for our respective routines if he moved to his own place. He did, around the corner, taking Reb on the weekends he wasn't working. This suited us, but a friend who was concerned about the impact our split living arrangements might be having upon our little girl, asked Reb where she lived.

'The kindie,' she said.

That did it. Reb's response prompted the decision for me to keep her with me full-time. Not quite the outcome either of us had had in mind, but it seemed the most sensible solution at the time. Reb and I were now effectively living on our own, although her dad visited when he had time.

Renovations continued unassisted. Soot from the 100-year-old rafters, discovered in a semi-drunken stupor the New Year's Eve I spent aloft (Reb was asleep) hammer in one hand, champagne in the other, yelling, 'What's so flippin' great about New Year's anyway?'

So too the smell of damp, rotten timbers and the oppressive presence of peeling paint, dinge and dilapidation, including bin bag after bin bag of clicking termite maggots found beneath the wall cladding.

Then there was the dust that blew in through the cracks in the walls and uncarpeted floorboards, and occasional dog plop stains on the floor (no matter how much I tried to dissuade), and child plop stains too – same difference. I'm sure Reb learnt this from the dog.

Finally, without a bathroom for three whole weeks and no running water for eight days, I found myself washing my sensitive bits in a dog bowl filled with cold, greasy water, and my spirit died. The struggle to live in an unfinished, grimy hovel won. I stopped trying to keep the house tidy, let alone vacuumed or swept, and I allowed the dog and my little girl to do whatever they liked. For work

I appeared normal – at home I was going round the twist.

Adding to my stress levels was my growing understanding of inner city living. Despite the cheek-by-jowl terraces, you never really saw or spoke much to neighbours – passers-by, yes – but neighbours tended to mind their own. I gradually figured out why; too much madness and mayhem.

Gang warfare and police raids on suspected criminals were quite common. One early morning bust resulted in a young chap having half his face blown off at point-blank range. There was also a fatal stabbing on the corner across from our home.

Robbery was almost de rigueur. One evening during dinner the terrace was broken into. I lost my jewellery. The thieves entered via the French doors to the bedroom. How they'd got up to the first floor balcony was a mystery – that was until I was shown photos of family gangs at the police station. Toddlers were hoisted onto their daddy's shoulders to climb over railings and slide through gaps in open windows or doors so they could rifle through others belongings, trained no doubt in what to take – money, wallets, anything shiny. The police noticeboard was covered. And these were the family gangs known to them.

Even the young bloke next door turned out to be a member of a gang of thieves. I'd heard them whistling to each other, and one night when I let the dog out I watched as he and two of his cronies trailed past my front gate with various car parts they'd just pilfered.

'Evening,' he said, smiling as brazen as you please.

Another night, after visiting a friend, I decided to walk home rather than take a taxi – it wasn't far. It was the small hours of Sunday morning and I met some of the night people: a chap sprouting long shaggy swathes of hair from beneath a hat crammed on his head and the ends of his sleeves shuffling along mumbling to himself (I couldn't bring myself to look at the bottoms of his trouser legs); folk, their faces burdened by disfigurement, who shied away from eye contact; demented souls engaged in intense monologues, shrieking and shouting; others pressed against walls seemingly terrified of any suggestion of physical contact.

I was particularly moved by the burly six foot four adult male in his forties, skipping along giggling and gurgling, to join his parents – easily in their seventies – to hold hands on a family walk under the kindly cover of darkness.

I mostly accepted what life was showing me – even the lady who tapped me on the shoulder as I waited in a bus queue to request that I kill her. I didn't, I swear.

However, the evening I sat down at my own dinner party and realised a complete stranger had joined the table marked the beginning of the end. As not all my guests knew each other I was introducing everyone. When I got to the chap I said, 'And you are?'

'Oh, you don't know me. I'm off the street. I saw you all from outside and you looked nice, so I climbed in through the window.'

I had bars fitted and decided it may be time to get away from city living. Needing bars to feel safe was not for me. At that point I'd been in Sydney precisely three years.

Despite the weird and wonderful predilections of the passing parade I also had the delightful, though admittedly occasionally distressing, distractions from my gorgeous young daughter to entertain me.

Exhausted by the relentless daily chores, I sometimes overslept having grouchily flicked off the alarm. Such was the case when I was roused from slumber by a male voice shouting from the street, 'Whose is this?'

Curious, I wandered onto the balcony to take a look and there was my twenty-month-old aloft in the hands of a taxi driver.

'She's mine!' I called.

'You'd better come and get her, love – she's a terrific traffic stopper.'

He was right. I could see the line of bumper-to-bumper cars snaking its way to Pyrmont.

How on earth did she get out? A set of kitchen steps, still at the scene, answered the question. Reb had dragged them from the kitchen, climbed on to reach the bolt at the top of the front door, and voila.

'She's alright,' said the taxi driver. 'I saw her playing in the gutter. Just glad you heard me.'

With that he gently but firmly handed me my bundle of joy and everyone resumed their day.

Another day, another late start. I lay awake listening for the telltale sounds from Reb's room, but there was silence. She must be downstairs. I didn't bother calling out as I figured she'd be curled up in front of the television, drawing or playing with toys. When I finally decided to rise and get a cuppa it was obvious she wasn't in the house. My anxiety level rose instantly. I checked the front door but it was securely bolted.

From the kitchen, I let myself out the back door, towards our bathroom that was still awaiting renovation. I heard muffled noises coming from within.

'Ah, there she is. What's she up to?' I said to myself.

As I crept towards the bathroom doorway, the head of my toddler covered in what looked like meringue peaks appeared and two round baby blues blinked from a little white face. We regarded one another. I didn't laugh – got very close – but that wouldn't have gone down well.

'What have you done to your hair?' I asked, completely baffled.

A slight movement of her arm exposed the petroleum jelly jar in her hand. She withdrew into the bathroom. I followed. There all was revealed; she was in the process of picking up the talcum powder container. Right. I get it. First rub in a fistful of jelly then liberally sprinkle with talc.

Forget D-Day. It was B-Day – Reb's long awaited second birthday. She was SO excited – had been for months. A party was planned and all her friends and favourite Sydney-based family members, including of course her daddy, were invited.

I'd bought sausage rolls, crisps, lollies and chocolate bikkies, cut cubes of cheese and vegetable sticks, put out dips and crackers, bowls of nuts and some fruit, plus the pièce de résistance – a Victoria sandwich, covered with butter frosting and chocolate freckles. Oh, and candles – mustn't forget the candles – all two of them!

Preparations aside, it was a fairly laid-back day. Reb was up at her usual time. She had a wash, ate brekkie, opened a couple of gifts from her daddy and me, watched a spot of telly, played with her toys and the dog, ate a light lunch and very deliberately positioned her seat (her potty chair minus the potty) in the middle of the lounge room. Shortly before the appointed hour, party hat on, Reb sat on her makeshift throne and awaited the arrival of her subjects – I mean guests.

The whole afternoon was a roaring success. Reb thoroughly enjoyed the meet and greet process, eagerly accepting and busily unwrapping the various gifts presented, kissing and hugging, in fact totally immersing herself in the adoration and attention of her fan base. All this time, she was totally nonplussed that she'd steadfastly remained – and had been from the time she'd got up – completely starkers.

On yet another pear-shaped morning, I awoke and sensed immediately that something wasn't right. Correctamundo – no Reb. This time she wasn't anywhere in the house. Now a lot more savvy to some of Reb's little ways, I checked the front door. It was shut but no longer bolted. Not again!

I panicked and glanced outside. She was nowhere in sight, just cars. It was 7.40am. Where was she? What if someone had taken her? Should I call the police? A report's got to happen quickly – isn't that what they say when a child goes missing? And you have to describe what they're wearing; I didn't know. I'd just woken up.

Anxiety-wracked, I wrapped myself in a towel – I was not about to waste time getting dressed, my daughter's life could be at stake. Ignoring the stares, I ran up the street and tore open the doors of the police station. There was no thought to wait my turn, I went straight to the desk sergeant. He heard me out, tried to reassure me and said that should I locate Reb to let him know.

In the meantime he'd put out an alert for a little girl answering my description – two years old, fine fluffy fair hair, big blue eyes, a turned up tip to her nose, rosy full cheeks, gorgeous smile, plumpish, about three feet tall, English speaking, with a pink strawberry shaped birthmark just above the nape of her neck. Tears welled in my eyes the whole time and there was a terrible age weary heaviness in my chest.

After telling me I'd done the best I could the desk sergeant offered me a cup of tea. I declined the offer and stumbled home, head reeling.

'Where was she?'

Back in the terrace I took a quick shower, dressed and attempted to have something to eat. The phone rang. Heart thumping I flew to it.

'Yes!' I snapped.

'Hi, is that you, Rhea?'

'Who's this?' I demanded. I didn't recognise the voice.

'It's your next-door neighbour.'

'Oh, hi,' I said, thinking, 'Not now!'

'I have something that belongs to you. Reb popped in earlier this morning. She told me you were sleeping so I kept her here, gave her some breakfast and waited 'til I thought you'd be up.'

It was now 9.20am.

'I'll be right round,' I said and promptly hung up.

Apparently Reb had opened the front door and it had closed behind her, so she'd actually done the most sensible thing. I thanked my neighbour for her hospitality towards Reb. I'm pretty sure the two of them had enjoyed a high old time while I'd been on the verge of a nervous breakdown.

Just then Reb emerged from my neighbour's kitchen and trotted along the hallway towards me. Beaming broadly, she chirped, 'Hiya, Mum.'

I bawled my head off.

One pleasant afternoon a few months later Reb wished to be involved in the action. I was in the backyard painting the wooden fence and had no objection to her watching, reasoning she'd soon lose interest, but why discourage curiosity? I asked her to fetch a brush from inside the bathroom. Happy to oblige, she trotted off out of view.

Mid-brush stroke I heard a huge gulping gasp, followed by the sound of a tin rolling on the floor. Then silence. I bolted to the bathroom.

My would-be helper was standing stock-still, her face, chest and shoulders were sunburnt red, her soft downy hair was plastered over her skull in oily strands, and her eyes were glazed. She had a brush in her hand. The one I'd been referring to still lay on the stool. She'd not seen that one but the handle of another, which was sticking out of a container of mineral turps on the table top.

Reaching for it, Reb had tipped the container's contents, which was a mixture of paint residue and turps, over her head. Not only had it burnt her skin, she'd swallowed some.

The initial shock over she burst into tears. I held her face beneath the bath's cold water tap. Understandably she freaked. Fighting me, I swaddled her in a towel and screamed for her dad, who was visiting us at the time, to call for an ambulance. Reb had become limp, her body succumbing to shock. I gently lay her down in the yard, knelt beside her and said over and over, 'Please don't die, baby. Please don't die.'

Her eyes fluttered shut.

We called the local hospital and were put through to Poisons who told us to clean as much of the paint off Reb as we could. We were then instructed to let her sleep and give her ice cream when she woke up. There'd be no need for an ambulance; she would be okay. She was, but that remains one of the worst moments of my life.

Not long after that my boyfriend, after consulting me, accepted a too-good-to-refuse offer of employment in Indonesia and our family dynamic changed once more.

Time marched on. Our bedrooms were now decorated – mine with pretty French blue Laura Ashley wallpaper, while Reb's was painted in light buttercup yellow with colourful friezes. Wall-to-wall carpet in the stairwell and the two living rooms downstairs gave an air of luxury, that and a proper back door. All that remained was the refurbishment of the kitchen and construction of a new laundry and bathroom, but the money for that was still a few work hours away.

One afternoon I was home early from work when I heard a demanding knock on the front door. I thought that one of the single mums must have dropped Reb home from kindergarten. But when I opened the door, I felt a child-sized determined shove on it. I stepped aside to let in a rosy-cheeked indignant individual with close-cropped light gold hair, dressed in pillar box red, corduroy dungarees, a white tee and leather sandals.

Eyes on mine, feet apart, hands akimbo, Reb demanded, 'Mum, what sex am I?'

A bit surprised by her question I answered simply enough, 'Female. Why?'

'What's with the dungarees and short hair?'

'Easier for me to keep you neat and clean.'

'Well, it's long hair and dresses from now on. Okay!?'

'Okay!' I said.

Gosh, what a little powerhouse. Memory of the force to be reckoned with, mentioned by the astrologer, stirred in my mind. I never did discover what had been said to light Reb's fire but lit it certainly was.

'I suppose you'd like to go shopping for a dress?' I asked.

I received a curt nod.

'Now?' I asked.

Another nod.

'Right!' I grabbed my purse and car keys. 'So you're going to grow your hair long?'

Curt nod number three. Message received and understood.

Slowly but surely the being that was my daughter was emerging.

Then, on a grocery trip to the local shops, with a grumpy, slightly resistant Reb in tow, I'd managed to keep our unit together – or so I had thought. It wasn't until the return journey that the cracks materialised. We'd rounded the corner, on the homestretch, me struggling under the weight of two enormous shopping bags on one side and Reb, hand in mine, on the other.

Suddenly, having decided she no longer wished to cooperate, Reb put on the brakes and refused to walk. I couldn't leave her so continued the battle, dragging her along the street as best I could.

She then started yelling, 'I want my mummy! I want my mummy!' I couldn't shut her up. What a total little cow! I was shocked. Here I was, doing my level best to be a loving mother, good friend and mentor to my offspring and this was where it got me.

'Shut up!' I hissed. 'I AM your mother,' I said as I wondered how I'd prove it if we were stopped by any passers-by. Talk about the tyranny of children – my child seemed effortlessly proficient. Scary!

Another revealing insight into Reb's personality came when I was upset at the plight of an injured pigeon I'd noticed, as we walked to kindergarten early one morning. Normally I'd make an effort to help a creature in distress, taking it to a vet. Not this day, as I didn't have time. Carefully picking it up, I gently hid it among some bushes and we continued on our way.

That evening, walking home with Reb I had a quick hunt for the pigeon, but couldn't find it. Once home, we ate tea and I tucked Reb into bed. However I couldn't get the injured bird off my mind.

Around 11pm we were back at the park in our nighties, slippers and raincoats. Holding a torch and her hand, I was haplessly fumbling about. After about ten minutes, Reb gave my hand a gentle squeeze and said, 'You know, Mum if you stop thinking about it the pain will go away.'

I stopped in my tracks, hearing the wisdom loud and clear. 'How do you know to say such things?' I asked.

She gently sighed, gave me a little smile and said, 'I just do.'

She was four. Still holding hands, we went home.

One flexi-afternoon about a year later, I was busy in my new kitchen. I'd been able to afford the refurbishment, which had been finalised courtesy of a bunch of contracted Italian labourers, and I loved how it had turned out. Instead of the dark, depressing hole it had been, light streamed in from a skylight and a new side window. The sink had been repositioned from its cramped spot in the corner to the middle of the kitchen divider overlooking the dining and lounge area. A slimline, double doored pantry and an overhead cupboard provided much needed storage space. I even had a mobile kitchen island and the new stove had pride of place in the refurbished fire alcove. It was lovely pottering about, lost in my own little world.

Around 2.30pm I thought I'd heard a knock at the front door. I peeked at the opaque glass panel in the top half of our also recently installed front door. No one. Knock knock. I looked towards the door again. As I still didn't see anyone I figured I'd imagined it. Less than a minute later there it was again. Knock knock. Curious, I walked to the door and opened it.

'Reb! What are you doing here? Aren't you supposed to be at school? And how did you get here?'

I was confused, these days I normally collected her in the car.

'I've been selling earrings on a stall. School finished early and I had nothing else to do, so the lady said I could help. Then I walked home. Don't worry, Mum I came along the backstreets 'cos I know you said main roads are dangerous.'

'What do you mean school finished early and what stall? And how did you cross the road? Oh, never mind. Give me your bag and come in.'

As we went into the kitchen I emptied her bag – lunchbox, pencils, toys, jumper, note. Note? The note, with last week's date, was informing parents of a pupil-free half-day. I didn't know whether to be cross or pleased. Now five, Reb didn't seem any the worse for her impromptu role as a street seller/lone ranger of the inner city Sydney suburbs and she definitely seemed resilient, if not resourceful. I was secretly very impressed.

At one point, Reb developed a habit of asking for a slice of cake and a carton of flavoured milk for breakfast at my favourite haunt, The Pudding Shop. Eating breakfast out was quicker and easier when I was working than faffing about at home, and initially I didn't mind. However she soon began selecting the most expensive slices, taking one bite and declaring, 'I don't like it.'

Determined this practice had to stop I told her the next time she chose cake I'd expect her to eat it.

The next day, Reb asked for a slice of a coffee and dark chocolate concoction, took one bite, looked me straight in the eyes and calmly announced, 'I don't like it.'

I took this as a deliberate challenge and stood my ground. Forty-five minutes of trickling tears and intermittent nose blowing later, there was half of it left. I would be running late for work at this rate.

'Right, Reb. We've got to go but you're taking the rest of the cake with you because it's going to be your lunch.'

More tears. More snot.

'I'm sorry, Reb, but I warned you.'

We got to the car, Reb clutching the crumpled paper bag containing the cake in her fist and still sniffling. But she could tell I wasn't going to back down. She then calmly enquired, 'If I eat a little more, will that do?'

'Possibly but it depends on what you mean by a little more.'

By the time we got to the school gate there was one fair sized chunk left – too big to ignore. She looked up at me. 'Do I really have to take this for lunch?'

'Yep.'

'Okay, wait a minute.' She shoved the remains into her mouth, swallowed and asked, 'Can I have lunch money?'

When Reb was approaching her sixth birthday she started talking about a party. As funds were low I ignored her hints thinking she'd forget about it and a birthday gift would do. Eight weeks passed and no further mention had been made. Great, the pressure's off. She's forgotten.

A few days before her sixth birthday, I received a pile of mail. Stooping to pick up the envelopes I noticed they were addressed to Miss R Wells. I was more used to 'Ms' but opened one anyway and read:

'Thank you, Reb, for inviting us to your party. We will be happy to bring $5. See you then, regards...'

'PARTY?' I opened the next one.

'Thank you, Reb, for the invite. $5 is fine...'

The remaining letters were all the same. I wasn't angry, just miffed.

'Reb!' I called, 'You've got some letters here and what's this about a party?'

'Oh yeah, 'cos you were busy I organised it myself,' she said.

'Where did you get the invitations and stamps?'

'Bought them.'

'And posted them?'

'Yep.'

'How long ago?'

'Three weeks.'

'How did you pay for them?'

'Pocket money.'

'But you've asked your friends to bring $5. You can't do that.'

'Why not? I told them you can't afford a party. I didn't think my friends would mind.'

I did a quick ring round to everyone saying not to worry about the $5, though most weren't fussed. Then I took off for the supermarket to stock up on some nibbles and drinks. Her party – why would I doubt it? – was a huge success.

Chapter Five

A Trial Run and European Fun

Thoroughly bored with life in Sydney it wasn't quite so easy to up sticks and move on any more. I held a permanent position, was a single parent of a schoolchild and was studying part-time. Wanderlust won the battle though and I decided that at the end of the Christmas period – when accommodation would be cheaper – we'd take the car and travel north. With only a week and severely limited funds the road trip was memorable for all the wrong reasons.

Impetuous as ever, I asked Reb if she fancied a drive, practically shoving her into the car along with our three-month old Labrador pup, Jack (Nanoo was no longer with us). Away we went, vague notions of Magnetic Island's palm trees and golden sands wafting about in my head. Three ten-hour driving days later we arrived in Queensland.

At the end of the second day on the road, Reb asked if she could have a swim in the hostel pool we were staying in. Initially reluctant as I was up to my armpits in soapsuds, doing dishes in the communal kitchen, I reasoned that, since the pool was in sight of the window, when I craned my neck, she'd be okay.

Pleased with my affirmative response, off she went. A couple of minutes later I could hear her joyful shrieks and giggles. Reassured, I got on with what needed doing.

Ten minutes later my focus was interrupted by an indignant little girl's voice – guess whose – yelling, 'What the hell do you think you're doing? You could've drowned me, you idiot!'

I stuck my head out the window. Reb was standing poolside,

hands on her hips, water streaming from her hair, giving a six foot chunk of Aussie male a right bollocking. Apparently she'd been balanced on his shoulders but floundered when he duck-dived. Unsure of what to do, she lunged forward, struggling to grab hold of the side of the pool. Not quite reaching – the idiot had hold of her ankles – she managed to kick herself free and was now giving him what for. Quite right, too.

The next day, tired after three days on the road and with only enough money for a room for one night, I booked us into a rundown motel on the outskirts of Townsville. Forget tantalising tropics, think dull disintegrating clapboard.

'But there's a pool,' I said, hoping to gee us both up.

We deposited our overnight gear and went to check it out. From the look of things it hadn't been serviced for years. Hundreds of dead bugs decorated the thick-looking, putrid water.

Reb took one look. 'We can't go in there, Mum.'

She was right. How disappointingly depressing. So close yet still so far from the palm trees and white sun-filled sandy beaches I'd been hoping to catch a glimpse of, but I'd reached my limit and wasn't going any further.

We had a weird night. We were the only patrons in the place, though hardly surprising considering. Come 8pm, the chap who'd booked us in was nowhere to be seen – probably had a luxury unit in town. His desertion meant I could easily smuggle Jack into the room as there was no one to complain or complain to. Still, it was worrying having a complete motel to ourselves. What if someone else rocked up? I decided to park my car out of view from the road. Thankfully, there were no disturbances and we ended up getting a reasonable night's rest, despite the humidity and struggling air conditioner.

The next morning the chap who'd booked us in was back at his post. He watched as we drove out but didn't say a word, so neither did I. Quite odd. Back on the road, day four of seven, we'd seen nothing and done nothing other than drive a huge distance.

Just out of Rockhampton, Jack fell out of the rear window when

I almost failed to negotiate a sweeping curve. He broke his leg and I broke my rule of never using my credit card. Jack's leg was splinted by a vet who agreed to open his surgery out of hours.

When we got back to Sydney nothing at home had changed, but we had. Jack was recuperating and Reb had developed the heebie-jee-bies about going anywhere with me in the car. As for me, I vowed any future trips were going to be a vast improvement on this one.

I enjoyed my job and loved being a mum but dearly wished to see the world and that wasn't going to happen unless I did something about it. Encouraged by a colleague, I decided to scratch my itch and take Reb backpacking overseas. She'd taken our earlier foray up north reasonably in her stride so I figured a world trip would do as much for her development as the equivalent time spent in school. Plus we wouldn't be going anywhere until an itinerary was planned and most accommodation booked – I'd already learnt that particular lesson.

Confident I could keep her up to speed with school work, should this be required, the education department wasn't too fussed about my taking Reb out of school, they actually supported my decision and wished us well on our future travels.

Leave confirmed and with everyone's blessing, six months later we boarded a plane for Austria. What we would be doing there I wasn't sure – it was in EUROPE, nothing else mattered.

After locating our seats – me by the window – Reb stood on hers to safely stow her dainty pink backpack, which contained her slippers and toothbrush. Wearing lightweight trackie pants, t-shirt and trainers, she was soon comfortably seated alongside me absorbed in her Game Boy and looking like the epitome of a six-year-old sea-soned traveller.

I projected cool, calm and collected in comfortable understated jeans and a casual open-necked shirt while butterflies flitted haphaz-ardly around in my stomach. I calmed down after take-off.

'Hey, Mum! Look! The world doesn't end at the edge of Australia!' Reb exclaimed.

We were several hours into the flight at this stage. Game Boy now turned off, the brilliantly clear sunny view had her attention as we flew over the coastline and Australia's sand-bordered land mass gave way to a sunlit ocean, sparkling far below.

'Yep. You're correct, Reb. The world doesn't begin and end with Australia. I'm glad you noticed.' It seemed taking off overseas was going to be a good thing.

Despite my nervousness about staying in a predominantly non-English speaking country we negotiated our arrival on European soil smoothly. A backpack each, nothing to declare and a handful of fellow travellers to jostle with, we were out of the airport in minutes.

Catapulted into a cold grey Viennese afternoon, with no familiar spots to loiter and no one we knew to loiter with, I consulted the Youth Hostels Association (YHA) guide. Within half an hour we were on board the designated tram, reassured and focused once more. During the twenty minute trip we were definitely an item of interest for several elderly commuters – most of whom were shabbily dressed. I was surprised by the stares and the state of their clothes. I smiled. No one reciprocated. Perhaps trams here were reserved for the poor and the aged, or a little girl travelling with her own backpack was unusual. Whatever. The natives so far didn't seem friendly. I stopped smiling.

Check-in time at the hostel was 4pm. At 2.30pm we had a snack, one of Reb's favourite pastimes (she's a Chinese Year of the Pig) in a nearby café, followed by supplies shopping. Several hours later, room secured, beds made, toiletries unpacked and zombie-tired, Reb's bedtime was looming and our evening meal was still on the agenda. Exploring would have to wait until the morrow.

We didn't hit the streets until almost midday and, unsure of my bearings, I decided not to wander too far. Besides, I had a little girl to consider. If Reb got overtired or anxious, the trip could become a nightmare. Keeping her contented meant our travels had to remain enjoyable. That was the plan.

With Reb's enjoyment uppermost in my mind, I treated her to time at a nearby fairground in Prater Park. She'd had a pony ride and a turn on the merry-go-round when I spied something a bit different – an extreme (there was the clue) experience simulator. That Reb's level of enjoyment wasn't my own escaped me. The big kid in me was excited that for a few schillings I could be in a rocket to the moon, on an F1 fighter plane, a Grand Prix racing circuit or skiing the Alps.

As Reb had asked about skiing, hearing about the Austrian Alps at school and here we were in Austria, I thought we could ski them with minimal outlay and none of the risks. It was the lure of a life-time. All we had to do was climb inside and go for the ride.

'Skiing. Dank u,' I said and paid the man.

Dutifully, Reb followed my lead and climbed into the four foot wide capsule. No windows, no straps, nothing to grip, just two bums on a short hard bench and a wrap-around video screen an arm's length away.

The door closed and we sat in the dark, breathing quietly. I was ready for action, though what Reb was ready for I honestly can't say. The video screen suddenly lit up with a breath-taking view of mountain tops and brilliantly glittering snow.

With milliseconds to visually orient ourselves, we quickly real-ised we were an extremely (there's that word again) long way up. The snowline on the screen moved up, out of view and we pitched stom-ach wrenchingly forward as we moved over smooth steep terrain.

After a few more seconds the snowline angled sharply to the side. Our seat, along with our view, tilted, twisted, dropped and jerked. So did we as we bounced and jostled roughly against one another.

'OOOF!' We were back on terra firma.

Then left, right, left again; we were still accelerating – how was that possible? We had no hope of doing anything but lean into the tight curves. Without warning the snow fell away again. With an almighty whoosh we were airborne, like the Olympic jumpers on the telly.

'Aaaaagggggghhhhh!' I gasped, hardly able to breathe.

Blood pounded in my ears. Once more the snow rushed up to greet us. Umph! Swish, swish, swish. Umph, thump! Forget the calm grace of the descent shown on the TV. This was a frantically frenzied, head first flurry of snow-flinging, face-stinging (well, it would have been if had it been real) free fall down a friggin' mountain.

Impact followed jarring impact as the bench pitched and gyrated beneath us like a mechanical bull those silly people in pubs try to ride, though they have an excuse – they're usually drunk.

'Wow! Isn't this great?' I yelled, my adrenalin having joined the party a while back.

There was no response. I glanced at Reb. She didn't look right. A mother knows these things.

Cheeks bulging ominously, lips tight, Reb turned her face towards me and gently shook her head. A tiny bubble of froth escaped the side of her mouth.

'Oh, Reb, I'm so sorry! Hold it, Bubs, please. You can't be sick in here. It's only a short ride. It'll be over soon. Can you hold it?' It was probably the longest three minutes of her little life.

All interest lost in skiing, I did my best to prevent poor Reb from spewing by covering her eyes with one hand and, in case of excessive spillage, putting the other over her own which was already covering her mouth. I held her firmly against me to reduce further movement.

She was white when the capsule came to a halt and all but fell out of the dratted thing. I expected her to hunch over and spill, but it didn't happen. Rock still, pale faced and teary, Reb looked mournfully at me. No sudden gush of vomit; the poor kid had swallowed it.

As a parent I was an abject failure. Day One not even half down and Reb was not having a good time, but as an adventure-seeking individual I was having a ball. After a quiet rest on a park bench I checked Reb was okay and offered the bribe of ice cream.

'Friends?' I asked.

A quick nod. Phew! Thank you, life.

The following day we took a train and got off at a little cement side-station in the middle of nowhere. The sign read, 'Wiennervald' – it looked like Vienna Woods to me. Two minutes later, in typical

European efficiency, the train departed and the platform was now as deserted as we were.

My watch read 7.30am. It was a cold, eerily quiet and foggy Sunday morning. What had possessed me to get us there so early? Trying to pack as much in as possible on a two-day flying visit probably. I was still surprised at our isolation though. I'd figured there'd be teeming masses of sightseers. I mean, wouldn't everyone want to be in the world-renowned Vienna Woods no matter what time it was? The die hard romantic in me was now struggling and under imminent threat – flight or fight?

We stood there, side by side, shivering as a vicious fog aggressively wrapped itself around us. We waited for five minutes – some less kind souls might say stupidly – for something to happen. Nada. Right. I had my answer. Fight.

I took Reb's hand and led her down the platform steps, and across the empty road towards the still sleeping houses. I had no idea where we were going as I didn't have a map. We may have been in or very near to the woods, I no longer cared. The initial excitement and enthusiasm had withered and died like autumn leaves in the forest we were still trying to locate. It was freezing and we were on foot, exposed and alone like the sole survivors of an apocalyptic event.

Cautiously wandering along hand in hand, I could sense Reb was unnerved by the stillness, so I decided to create a bit of light-hearted magic and mystery. The quaint cobbled streets, thatched roofs and latticed windows provided the perfect setting.

'Reb, see that pointed roof?' I asked as a black slate turret rose sharply above the house diagonally ahead of us.

'Yes,' she said.

'Who do you reckon might live there?'

'Where? In the turret?'

'Yeah…maybe a witch?' I said, my voice breaking; its pitch more piercing than I'd intended. It must have been all the excitement.

'A witch?' she squealed.

A momentary flash of alarm sparked in her eyes but a quick glance

49

at mine, plus a squeeze from my hand reassured her sufficiently. She hardly missed a beat.

'Yeah, could be a witch's place,' she said.

I pointed to a blackbird perched on the roofline and said, 'If it was, do you think that blackbird might be her messenger?'

'Yeah. A bird would make a good messenger, wouldn't it, Mum?'

Right on cue the blackbird took flight.

'Do you think it heard us? Maybe it's gone to tell the witch there are strangers in town. Let's watch where it goes.'

The bird flew one rooftop further on, landing with a confidently cackled caw and turned to watch us, head slanting from side to side; all beady bright-eyed birdy curiosity.

Attention now divided between the roofline and the path, we managed to follow the twisty laneway, occasionally slipping but with no accompanying giggles – this was a sincerely sober business – through the postcard-like village.

Rain came and went in a matter of minutes, but there was enough to create shallow puddles. Following a brief interlude it started again, water droplets stirring the puddle surfaces as if tiny people were swan diving from a great height.

'Hey, Reb,' I said, indicating the splashes, 'Fairies.'

'Yeah,' she said, entranced.

By this point her pupils were enormous. She had also slowed to a tentative, tiptoed creep, taking care not to step in any puddles yet wired for blackbirds, turrets and black cats. Every now and then she'd pull me towards her and whisper her observations in my ear, and I whispered mine back.

We stayed like this for half an hour until, at the end of the main street, bored with our game and feeling a bit peckish, we turned our backs on the quaint hamlet and returned to the station. With any luck a train would soon arrive and deliver us by brunch time.

On the return trip Reb slept solidly, her cheek pushed flat against the window, her soft lips squished into a puckered cupid's bow. She was a sweet but not so little (she liked her food, remember) cherub.

As I gazed at the passing vista I noticed a couple of ponies on the far side of a mist shrouded paddock. One was silver and one blue (mist will play tricks) and I know this is poetic licence, but it looked like they had nodules on their shoulders. When Reb woke I mentioned the ponies to her.

'Were they really silver and blue?' she asked.

'The way I saw them they were.'

'What were the nods…nods…knobs on the their shoulders for?'

'Maybe that's where their wings will grow,' I replied.

She squeezed my hand and smiled, and I squeezed hers back. Our trip to Vienna Woods was etched in our memories for the rest of our lives.

Refreshed from our rest on the train and tummies full, that afternoon we visited the St Petersburg salt mines. I don't remember how we got there but I do remember donning full length, white hooded overalls before sitting astride a polished wooden beam and sliding majestically, seventy metres to the bottom – not a splinter in sight – from where the assembled huddle of tourists embarked on a short walking tour. It was an unexpected and amusing introduction to life in the salt mines, but the gloss well and truly came off at the conclusion of the tour when we had to climb several lengthy sets of stairs to get out.

From Austria we travelled First Class using Aussie-issued Eurail passes (it was definitely one of my best travel investments) across Germany. We visited Nuremberg where Reb was fascinated by a poor pig's decapitated head on a platter in a butcher's showcase.

That night we slept in a gloriously airy room in the comfiest bed ever, enveloped in masses of pristine white swishy swansdown duvet. Wonderful.

The next day's train travel took us through Cologne, of which neither of us remembers anything other than some imposing spires, before eventually being deposited in Holland. We were due that evening at a friend's – Tessa – whom I'd met some years back while living in Sydney.

En route I developed a terrible toothache. With one side of my face threatening to become melon sized, I gave up my usual stoicism and purchased painkillers at a station chemist. They kind of worked; the pain came and went in blinding waves for the remaining six hour journey while Reb occupied herself playing cards with fellow travellers.

Upon our arrival in Den Haag (The Hague) and still desperately wanting the intense aching to cease, but not wishing to miss out on anything, I treated myself to a Pilsner. Well, I bought it thinking I'd drink it later that evening at my friend's by way of celebration.

Great idea. I threw it up within half an hour of downing it (medication and alcohol always a great mix) all over Tessa's bedding. Thankfully Tessa wasn't in yet, having kindly left her spare key with the instructions to make ourselves at home. I seemed to be doing that well enough!

I put Reb to bed and then, in a teary, chemically-induced migrainous haze, cleaned up as best I could. As there was no bucket anywhere that I could see, I eventually located a deep sided ceramic bowl, just in case.

My host returned at midnight after a long day at work and was unsurprisingly unimpressed at the stench and condition of her apartment. However, as a good friend will, she listened to my predicament and came up with the obvious solution. First thing in the morning she would ring her dentist. She did as promised. By 12.45pm the offending tooth, with its ugly black root was in a bin. Wonderfully, I was now pain free to go where the wind blows. I LOVE Tessa AND that dentist in Holland.

A friendship with Anna, a Swedish backpacker I'd met in Tasmania a few years earlier on another of my solo trips (Reb stayed with my sister for the duration) led to our being invited to her parents' potato and strawberry farm near Mariestad.

The trip across from Holland, which took in the whole of Denmark, was unremarkable. We had overnight sleeper berths which guaranteed, at that time of year, that we saw nothing. It was dark when we boarded and dark when we disembarked. It was therefore great to be greeted by my friend's bright sunny smile and her equally happy parents Kristen and Olaf.

A delightfully hospitable couple, Kristen and Olaf were very loving and family-orientated. Olaf took an instant shine to Reb who became a surrogate granddaughter to dote on for a few days. He told her he'd take her elk hunting. I wasn't one hundred per cent sure he was serious but didn't know enough about the ways of Swedish folk to question his announcement.

I just smiled and said, 'You hear that, Reb? We're going elk hunting.'

'What's an elk?' she asked.

'It's kind of a big deer with huge antlers.'

'What are antlers?'

'You know. The things on top of the heads of Father Christmas' reindeer,' I said.

'Oh. Elk hunting!' she exclaimed knowingly, like she'd misheard. We all laughed.

At dinner everyone, including me (and I was used to Reb's love of food), was impressed by her appetite. She had three full helpings of potato, out-eating everyone at the table including Olaf's strapping teenage sons, further amazing Olaf when she still had room for dessert.

The following day, cold and overcast, we were ferried by family car to the edge of an Icelandic lake. Reb rugged up in a borrowed fur lined parka and I, in a borrowed raincoat, boarded Olaf's motorboat.

Within minutes we were skimming speedily across a huge expanse of grey water. Wind whipping her hair, Reb did her best to keep a look out for elk, although the shore was some distance away. We were perhaps figuratively, as well as literally, being taken for a ride, but it was with such pleasant company.

A week later, back in Holland, Reb the budding socialite demanded she sit inside at the bar and grill for lunch where the adults sat, instead of outside at a sidewalk table. Leaving her for a minute, I approached the barman – a tall, amicable, pretty, blonde young man – and told him of Reb's request.

'Vell, obviously I won't be serving her alcohol, but if she sits at the end of the bar I can't see there being a problem,' he said in a heavy Dutch accent.

I beckoned Reb over. She keenly clambered aboard a stool, teetering on it unsteadily towards the bar. I repositioned her so she could lean on the counter without toppling over.

'And vhat vould you like, mevrouw?' the attractive barman asked.

'A milkshake,' Reb confidently replied.

'Vun milkshake coming up,' he said as he departed to do her bidding.

'Mum,' she declared swivelling round to face me, eyes wide, 'That man's wearing make up.'

'Yep. He is. Does it suit him?'

'Yes.'

'Well, that's okay then,' I stated.

Reb's introduction to the world at large looked set to continue.

A couple of nights later, Tessa invited us both out to dinner. It was a matter of great excitement, but what to wear? Tessa, a professional costume designer at the time, had an extensive and exclusive range to choose from. I was easily fixed and selected a stunning silver and turquoise shot silk shirt. My outfit was much easier than kitting out a six-year-old wannabe fashionista.

With only half an hour until our departure, Reb was decidedly dejected. She wanted to look gorgeous too, but how? Everything was way too big – Tessa stood over six feet tall in her stockinged feet.

Satisfied with her appearance – I was still faffing about – Tessa focused on Reb. Rummaging through her gear she pulled a few blouses from her collection. The shiny tartan-esque Thai silk taffeta number in muted hues of lilac, green and pink caught Reb's eye.

A few well-placed pins, plus a silk scarf cummerbund later, Reb was resplendent in a three-quarter length 'dress coat'.

Hair issues too were resolved by Tessa who, with a few timely tips from Reb, successfully braided her blonde locks. Looking good!

What about the finishing touches? Riffling through an assortment of costume jewellery produced a pair of clip on earrings – huge gilt bows with tear-shaped drops – perfect as far as Reb was concerned.

Now her nails. Too easy – twenty shades available. Bright red will do nicely, thank you.

What about shoes? Reb's sneakers didn't work with her new-found glamour. Besides, she wanted heels, I knew. After a flurried five minute search in the bottom of Tessa's wardrobe we all agreed on a low heel pair – way too big really, but Reb could at least manage to shuffle along, if not exactly walk.

Finally, lipstick for good measure. An evening bag clutched firmly in her hand we made our departure, all totally gorgeous and ready for a night on the town.

Chapter Six

London, Nan and Pop, and the Hawaiian Sun

Our two-week stay flashed by. We'd had a lot of fun but it was now time to fly to London before heading onto Scotland to visit Nanna and Pop.

Day one of our six-day stay in London was spent taking in London's major attractions on the red double decker buses.

'You'll love the buses, Reb. They're fun. They've got tight twisty stairs and huge windows to see everything,' I said.

We bought our tickets from the conductor, a proud Cockney who dispensed them with a flourish from an old fashioned ticket machine.

'That'll be three pound fifty pee for you, Missus,' …whirr click, whirr click… 'An' two pound fifty pee for the nipper,' …whirr click.

Our seats were up top at the front. They were perfect until it started raining.

'I can't see anything, Mum,' Reb whined every few seconds.

I pretended not to hear her until, at the last of the rained-out drop-off spots near St Paul's Cathedral, Reb declared, 'I'm bored. I want to do something else.'

My wily endeavour to do what I wanted while masquerading it as something she would enjoy was foiled already. In fact, our earlier walk beneath Big Ben had failed miserably too.

'It's a clock, Mum. A big clock,' she said. The disappointment and frustration with her mother's choice of fun activities clearly evident.

How about the Tube then? London's underground rail system which endlessly ferries commuters between famous destinations such as Bond Street, Charing Cross, Earls Court, Kew Gardens and

London Bridge seemed much more to Reb's Capricornian, cosmopolitan liking. Plus the escalators released fond memories for me of a trip I'd made, aged eight, to the children's exhibition at Olympia in London with my dad.

Reb was further impressed by a band of colourfully clad Jamaican buskers. A gently intoned, 'Here ya go,' accompanied the dropping of a few coins in their collection tin.

After an hour without daylight, the demand, 'Now where?' came.

'Buckingham Palace?' I said.

'What's that?'

'It's where the Queen lives. If the flag's flying, she's in.'

'Okay. I wanna see.'

But the trip to the Queen's London pad was postponed until the next day as we'd both had enough of the rain.

Our second, pleasantly sunny day found us gawking – not much else we could do – outside the gates of Her Majesty's abode, surrounded by her fellow serfs. There was a subtle stirring as the main gates were opened, followed by a general commotion as a group of regimental soldiers marched, surprisingly noiselessly, towards them. They continued through and veered in perfect formation right in front of us.

Reb was intrigued by their busbies.

'They're made of bear fur,' I said.

'Are there bears in England?'

My comment of, 'Not any more. They killed them all to make their hats,' received such a look of outrage I rescued the situation by declaring, 'Only kidding!'

Later we checked out the Horse Guardsmen in their sentry boxes. I mentioned their not being permitted to move while on duty.

'Not even blink?' asked Reb.

'No. Not even.'

Ending up in St James' Park, we fed the birds, the sparrow-sized jackhammer blows from their tiny beaks insistent on our outstretched palms. Reb also had a go at feeding family-orientated ducks, snooty malevolent swans and dive bombing, pillaging pigeons before giving up. There was too much violence.

At the halfway mark on day three, we paid a flying visit, not my intention, to the Victoria and Albert Museum. Reb's enchantment with the Queen's gold carriage lasted barely three minutes before I read the signs.

'Next?' I queried.

A swift nod.

A brief Tube ride permitted us to pop up outside The Royal Opera House in London's Covent Garden. It had taken twenty-one years for me to actually be there and precisely twenty-one seconds to hear, 'Seen it. Now where?' Reb's lights had gone out.

'How about Harrods?' I said. However when we actually arrived, I added, 'Completely overpriced.' Reb's comment, 'Boring!' Fortnum and Mason's? (What was I thinking?) Reb's comment, 'Boring!'

'C&A Mode's kid's department?'

BINGO, on both accounts. I'd promised Reb a nice outfit for when she visited her grandparents and we'd be there soon. After an hour's happy hunting, we selected a smart black and white dress with a black bow at the neckline and matching waistcoat, a black and gold headband, and black pumps. Very chic!

On a roll, I impulsively bought tickets to the Sadler's Wells matinee performance of *Cinderella* in the West End for the following afternoon.

The theatre was a dinky, antiquated steeply-tiered affair, all gilt and heavy drapes, dating from way back when. Seated on the third tier, our knees were level with the tops of the heads of the audience members in front of us. We felt that toppling over when standing was a definite possibility, but the ballet was a success. Totally entranced by the comic genius of the two ugly sisters, Reb's lights came back on. Mine too.

On our last day, we located Petticoat Lane Market where a woman wanted to sell us an 'Amazing Clucking Chicken' for a pound. This was a tin can with a piece of string threaded through a small hole which, when successively jerked, sounded – you guessed it – just like a chook. I'd have paid her a pound for a picture of her pulling on the clucker but she refused to cooperate, so I snapped her when she wasn't looking.

Later that afternoon we packed our bags ready for our departure for Scotland the following day. Ours wasn't a fancy hotel – I'd taken the cheapest I could find. It had two single beds, a chair, wardrobe, basin and mirror, and we had to wait our turn to use the bathroom and shower. As for the loo, that was one floor down and along the corridor, which was fine in daylight hours but decidedly creepy in the dead of night. Besides, there was no way I'd leave Reb sleeping alone to visit the toilet, so I peed in the sink. Very awkward, I can tell you! I thoroughly rinsed the sink though and even poured a bit of perfume in – the perfect use of *eau de toilette, tu ne crois pas*?

Having caught our train on time we were now due at my parents' Scottish hometown of Hawick where they'd retired from South Australia. A matter of great anticipation, Mum and Dad had not seen me or their granddaughter since she was two, almost five years ago. Too long, but circumstances dictated all the terms.

Mum's health issues had forced my folks to relocate to the only cold climate they knew – Mum's country of origin – where a pensioner flat was also available. Plus, as a professionally paid but part-time employee and single parent, taking such a trip had been financially impossible for me until now.

It was an overcast chilly afternoon when our train pulled into Carlisle Railway Station in England – the closest station to Hawick – twenty minutes late. Due to the bulkiness of my backpack we tended to be the last off most trains, as it was easier than struggling against the crush. Today was no different even though we were both incredibly excited to see my mum and dad.

As we followed the crowd, a slightly-built, well dressed, kindly-looking and thoroughly wrinkled elderly lady made her way towards us smiling and waving.

I said to Reb, 'Isn't that nice? Someone's grandma's come to meet them,' glancing behind me to see who the recipient was. No one was there. Someone's grandmother had indeed come to meet them – Reb's.

'Mum?'

'Who else?' she said in that slightly frosty, matter-of-fact air she'd always had about her.

I wrapped my arms tentatively around her. This woman was tiny. A little bird of a thing. She disappeared inside my embrace and her diminutive frame felt incredibly fragile. I'd have crushed her as easily as eggshell if I squeezed the tiniest bit. That time is a truly sneaky companion to us all was, from that moment, forever fixed firmly in my mind.

I let Mum go and waited. Reb, less in awe of the situation than I was, didn't hesitate. She took her grandmother's hand and the three of us walked off, chatting quietly, to locate Dad who'd gone to park the car.

When we descended the ramp over the railway lines he came into view, beaming. He'd lost a bit more hair, walked a little more stiffly and had a bit of a tummy – something he would never have tolerated in his younger years – but other than that he still looked like Dad.

Rebecca ran up to him for a cuddle calling happily, 'Hiya, Pop!'

'Hiya, Reb,' he said. 'Hello, Andy love,' he said to me.

I was always Andy to Dad (shortened form of Andrea) and that had always remained special.

Discovering that children in Hawick traditionally attended Guy Fawke's night in fancy dress (only a week away), Reb immediately announced she'd be going as Raphael, her favourite Teenage Mutant Ninja Turtle (TMNT). The first TMNT craze had hit while we were in Holland. As luck would have it, I'd already bought a Raphael doll – part of Reb's forthcoming Christmas present. Mum had no idea what TMNTs were or what Raphael looked like, so I snuck her a look.

A clothing hunt then ensued among our collective wardrobes – this was getting repetitious. Thank goodness I had the doll to refer to – once Reb made her mind up, look out. By the end of that particular afternoon we'd pretty much covered all bases. Red scarf/mask – check. Red top warm enough for outside – check. Red trews (trousers) tucked into a pair of Mum's suede boots – check. Was there any need for a cape? Nah. What about a sword? Not really

– she just needed to strike a fencing stance and have an aggressive facial expression.

Reb looked great and thoroughly enjoyed playing with all the kids at the local bonfire, eating the tablet (fudge) Nanna had made specially, and giggling gleefully each time Pop handed her more sparklers. I was warm and glowing too. It was good to feel so at ease, so at home.

The six weeks with my folks went by pretty quickly. In that time we celebrated Mum's seventy-first birthday, my thirty-sixth and our first Christmas together as a family.

On Christmas morning Reb woke me at 4am, unable to contain her excitement. As Nan and Pop were still sleeping, I convinced her to resist opening her presents. They would, I knew, love to watch her opening her gifts. She negotiated opening half.

Dad was next up. He was not much of an early riser these days, but having his youngest daughter and youngest grandchild visiting at Christmas was a rare and special event. After Reb opened a couple more gifts – she had been royally spoilt, Dad started preparing breakfast and suggested Reb and I wash and dress ready for when Mum made her appearance. Mum didn't sleep too well at night these days, so often got up later in the day. We did as he asked.

Eventually the four of us, dressed in the equivalent of our Sunday best, sat down to a full brunch of egg, bacon, tomato, fried bread, tea, toast and marmalade, after which Reb opened the remainder of her gifts.

Just before we were due to return to Oz, Reb announced, 'I want to go home.'

I suspected she'd run out of emotional and physical puff.

'You've got your wish, Reb. We leave in three days, though we'll be stopping in Hawaii for your birthday. How's that?'

Reb looked relieved and pleased. For a little tacker she'd done well. She'd taken almost three and a half months of travelling in her stride, but she'd reached her limit. I was chuffed we'd got as far as we had. Three days later, just before Reb's seventh birthday, we were in an Hawaiian hotel overlooking the ocean.

Reb, no longer interested in sightseeing, wanted to lie around in her iridescent, purple bikini – one of her Christmas presents, and play on her Game Boy. I'd hoped she'd forgotten about it. Fat chance.

In an attempt to motivate her, I asked how she wanted to celebrate her birthday and was surprised when she said she wanted to go to Hungry Jacks in a limo. Hungry Jacks I could do, it was around the corner, but a limo? I rang the concierge of our hotel and was put in touch with a car hire company. It cost $50 for half an hour. Low on funds, I hesitated. When I was asked to confirm the destination and number of passengers, I revealed it was my daughter's seventh birthday and it was her wish to ride to Hungry Jacks in a limo. I heard, 'Leave it with me. I'll arrange something. Be ready for 7pm tomorrow.'

Slightly ahead of the appointed time, Reb and I took the lift to the lobby and went out the front, as instructed, to where a huge, white, gleaming stretch limo was waiting. The driver's door opened and a smiling, slightly-built Japanese woman, wearing a chauffeur's cap approached and checked our names.

'Yes, we're the Misses Wells.'

'Please get in,' said the female chauffeur. I hadn't expected that. Before we climbed aboard I confirmed the cost.

'You spoke with my husband. The hire cars are his business and rather than send an official driver he sent me. The charge is $US4 to go to Hungry Jacks.'

I was touched that the owner of the company had arranged this and hoped his wife hadn't been too put out. We climbed in and Reb had another taste of the high life in a four minute four dollar ride around the block, surrounded by tinted glass, polished wood, luxurious leather and brass fittings.

The next day Reb was feeling sorry for me so she found me a companion, a female sun worshipper she'd befriended two minutes prior.

Lying on the sand, engrossed in a book, I sensed I was no longer alone. The sun in my eyes, I recognised Reb's outline but felt compelled to stand as she introduced me to an overly made up, bronzed blonde six-foot-two Glamazon, a shade this side of fifty in a bikini-thong and not much else.

My God her mammary glands had to be plastic, didn't they? Reb introduced her beach buddy and disappeared – good deed done.

'Pleased to meet you,' I stammered.

Now what? There was an awkward silence, which was thankfully short-lived as the woman turned and waved to someone.

'Yoohoo!' she called out. 'That's my hubby. He'll be wondering where I've got to. Nice meeting you.' She sauntered off and didn't return. Thank you, life.

Chapter Seven

Back in the Land of Oz – Playing Pirates

Upon our return to Australia we stayed with friends in Bondi. It was nice taking time out in their apartment, two blocks from the famous beach, though I soon lost interest in trying to be trendy, worrying about my appearance, brand of sunglasses, or the depth of my tan in the fashionable seaside suburb.

After a couple of months I decided to swap city chic for coastal calm, taking up another friend's invitation to stay on his yacht. Although possessive of his privacy, I suspected the offer was extended in part due to an impromptu and, as it turned out, unnecessary rescue mission I'd attempted prior to going overseas when I'd thought my friend was in trouble.

By 10.30pm on the evening in question, I was worried by his failure to call me as was his custom. Aware he'd been complaining of arm and chest pains, I left Reb with my neighbour and drove the thirty kilometres to where his boat was moored, one hundred metres offshore.

Midnight found me groping in the depths of the cabin, virtually naked and flippin' freezing. I lurched and fell forward, my deathly cold, wet hand finally finding something familiar – no, not that – my friend's face as he lay sleeping.

'What the?!' he spluttered, waking. 'Who? What the heck?'

'Shhh. It's me,' I said.

'What are you doing here in the middle of the night? And more to the point, how did you get here?'

He was incredulous.

'I swam.'

'You swam?! But why? It's the middle of the night!'

'I know,' I said, 'but you didn't ring. I thought something had happened to you, so instead of sitting around wondering, I came to find out. I called your name a couple of times from the shore, but decided since the yacht wasn't too far out I may as well swim the rest of the way.'

'But how did you get on board? And where did you leave your clothes?' he asked, his voice getting higher.

I could hear his thoughts, 'Was this woman in command of her faculties?'

'I climbed into the dinghy and pulled myself along. My clothes are on someone's jetty and you can think what you like but I'd do the same for any of my friends if I thought they were in trouble.'

'I wouldn't,' he retorted, but I could tell he was impressed.

So Reb and I got several weeks free board up north while he completed his preparations for a solo cruise.

One thundery evening the three of us were sitting in my Volkswagen trying to accommodate each other. We'd been guests a week already when, out of a sense of instilling some fun and excitement, we'd driven to the local point to watch a summer storm. Massive, dark clouds loomed closer and gentle splatter was suddenly replaced with torrential rain. Despite being warm and sticky we enjoyed watching one of nature's most exhilarating displays of power.

Curious, I embarked on a series of questions which, more than anything else, revealed my total ignorance of the elements to our seafaring companion.

Quite innocently I enquired, 'Does the yacht have a lightning rod?'

'Yes,' he said quickly.

'Where is it?'

'It's called the mast,' came the mocking reply, a little twinkle glimmered in his eye.

'Oh,' I said, miffed. I struggled on. 'Well, what happens if the yacht is struck by lightning?'

'The likelihood of that happening is remote.'

I tried again.

'Would you be at greater risk at sea?' I asked.

'I suppose so.'

I left it at that. It didn't pay to push my friend's tolerance of ignorance too far.

Following a further couple of night's extreme electrical activity, my friend decided to move his craft. He went below decks to warm the engine.

'That's strange,' he said, 'The ammeter shows full charge and the needle's bent. It should show zero.'

He mentioned he hadn't been sure of the ammeter's accuracy but it was supposed to be the best money could buy. He removed the unit and fixed it.

After re-berthing, he was sitting on the deck when he happened to glance at the mast. Something was wrong.

'Why's there a hole?' he mused.

Puzzled, he walked over to check it out. On further reflection he realised there was no antenna. After mumbling something to me, he tried his beautiful, new, pride and joy, high-tech sea phone. Nothing. Dead as a dodo. Unconvinced, he tested the electrics to no avail. He checked the fuse, it was completely blown.

'Mmm…it looks like we were struck by lightning,' he said. 'Now I know why the ammeter showed maximum deflection. The power surge would have forced the needle completely off the dial and its extraordinary reading indicates where it was deflected to.'

A typical Sagittarian in such matters I sought the bottom line. 'It was bounced,' I said.

'Yeah, that's right,' he replied.

The final piece of the puzzle had still to fall into place. When had this occurred? The previous night we'd been on board so it couldn't have been then, as surely we'd have noticed.

'It must've been when we were on the point,' my friend concluded, 'About the same time you asked me if boats ever get hit by lightning!'

One exceedingly hot afternoon, Reb and I arrived back at the boat harbour heavily laden with provisions. I called out expectantly. No answer. I called again. No response. That's odd. He must be on board; the dinghy's alongside. Probably asleep, though he'd normally wake at the slightest disturbance. I tried again. More silence.

It's amazing how the frustration caused by the separation of a fifty metre stretch of water can instantaneously convert into pure hysteria, especially when you're me.

'Gee, Reb, he's been complaining of a sore arm recently,' I said as I thought how sore arms can be linked with heart attacks. 'I hope he's alright. I could swim out I suppose.'

I'd done it before but I knew a massive stingray cruised these particular waters.

I stood motionless as I squinted into the sun, my arms straining under the weight of the shopping bags. I thought about the earlier training from my boat-mad friend – don't get the bags wet and no sand either. As I waited, watching for signs of life, the internal alarm bells began to win. He must be on board, but why isn't he answering? Something must have happened, surely?

I called again. Nothing doing.

'Oh, come on, Mum, let's go,' Reb moaned, 'I'm thirsty and I want to get out of the sun.'

'Two more minutes,' I answered, 'Then we'll go.'

But where? I thought. I know. Air Sea Rescue.

Two minutes later we were on course for their HQ. On arrival I told my story.

'Can you help?'

'Of course,' the burly gentleman replied. 'You never know, it could be serious. Besides, it's better to be safe than sorry.'

Back at the yacht no one spoke as they appraised the situation. Then the older of the two chaps who'd followed Reb and me to the mooring told his companion, 'Take off your jeans and swim for it.'

Simultaneously, the young man let out an ear-splitting whistle. Thirty seconds later, there in the hatch, rubbing his eyes, scratching other bits and yawning, appeared my companion. 'What's up?' he called.

'Nothing now,' I mumbled, sheepishly.

'Air Sea Rescue, mate,' replied the other man.

My companion frowned and went below deck. The two blokes, all smiles, made their way back to their vehicle, got in and disappeared. Being friendly with a salt of the earth yachtsman can have embarrassing ramifications, not only for the yachtsman.

Upon our return to Sydney a few months later, having finally experienced and thoroughly enjoying our stay in a palm-fringed, white sand tropical paradise, I was given the option of resuming my previous posting or taking a new one up north. This was an unexpected but welcome development.

'How far up north?' I asked.

'The mid-coast of Northern New South Wales.'

'Which is where?' I asked.

She hesitated. Hint one. She told me and hesitated again. Hint two. Ever the optimist, I jumped at the chance to leave Sydney.

'Yep, I'll go,' I said.

'Are you sure?' Hint number three. 'You don't want to think about it overnight and give me your answer tomorrow?' Hint number four but still no alarm bells.

'No, I'll only lie awake all night mulling. I'll go' I said.

'Okay. Report to work this Monday.'

Eek, less than a week's time!

My previously stored furniture – from before our three-month stint overseas – remained so, and three days later Reb, my pooch, and I, in our aged Volksie packed to bursting, trundled onto the Pacific Highway for yet another lengthy road trip. After numerous loo stops, another overnight stay in a motel plus a top speed of forty-five kilometres an hour, we crept into our destination late the following afternoon.

Having driven along the shoulder for almost the entire distance of 625 kilometres, we finally attracted the attention of a traffic cop. He pulled me over and said, 'Excuse me, Madam is there a reason you're driving so slow?'

I didn't have the nerve to tell him if I drove any faster the

V-dub started to shake so hard things threatened to fall off. Instead, I told him a different truth. I was moving house. He'd already noted the contents of the car which were packed level with the bottom of the windows – even the dog had been wedged into place, I kid you not!

'Do you have far to go?'

'No, only three kilometres,' I said.

I wasn't lying. We were moving house and I was three kilometres from our rural New South Wales destination. I'd just driven past a tourist information board telling me so.

'Right. On you go then.' The cop followed us for a few minutes but when I turned onto the main street he lost interest.

I secured a place for us to live by enquiring at a community centre. As luck would have it, one of the staff members was looking for someone to share her place with. We moved in – it would have to do until I had time to find something better.

Reb was enrolled at the public school that Monday morning and I started my new job directly after the event.

Chapter Eight

Bali Time and Chicago Crime

Despite an initial relatively calm adjustment period, life's universal intelligence still determined that our lives would remain far from dull or boring. So about a year later, after comfortably settling in, I decided to take Reb, now almost eight, to Bali for our Christmas vacation. Her dad still lived there and she'd not been in his company since she was a toddler.

Upon our arrival we took a cab to the resort he was working at and enjoyed a few days mixing it with the twenty-something Aussie patrons. Reb, taking it all in her stride as usual, slotted herself right in, making friends with her dad's work colleagues as readily as she befriended him. Although a veritable stranger this was of no consequence to Reb – he was her dad and the two of them took up where they left off.

A couple of nights later we moved to a less drunken orgy, more family-orientated establishment. Feeling like we'd not stopped for days, it was heaven to collapse in the late afternoon onto a big ornately-carved bed, even if the room did smell a bit musty, and dissolve into sleep.

I jolted awake in the darkness. Something was making its way over the bedcovers. A fairly solid something, moving along the line of my outstretched leg. A rat? I threw the bedclothes off. Reb was lying next to me and didn't stir, even when whatever it was hit the far wall of the room with a hefty thud.

I reached for the bedside lamp and switched it on. Glistening in the lamplight was the remains of our foil-wrapped tomato sandwiches her dad had given us. They'd been gnawed to bits. I was not impressed. $US50a night for rats? Not bloomin' likely.

The following morning I crossed the road from the hotel and enquired about a homestay with a Balinese family. For four Aussie dollars we could have our own apartment, not just a room. For a further two dollars a day we could access the hotel's swimming pools as well as frequent their restaurants. I much preferred this arrangement.

Our new private digs had a mezzanine bed space for Reb, a single bed for me, a waist height, concrete block bathing cubicle (or mandi) in one corner, a separate loo, loads of shelving housing loads of interesting looking books, and an outdoor shower. Waking up to a glorious day, I decided to get up rather than laze.

Toiletries and towel in hand, I pushed through the swing doors to the shower when a plate-sized frog, dislodged from its perch, landed on my head. At least it wasn't a rat!

One evening during our six-week stay I convinced Reb, who was not always inclined towards excessive exercise, to walk into town to an eatery we'd not been to before.

This particular restaurant had an outdoor section with tables and chairs around a central pond housing luxuriant floating leaves of perfectly formed water lilies. Making ourselves comfortable, lemonade for Reb and a cocktail for me, I'd taken a book out and agreed to Reb amusing herself in the garden-like confines.

Mesmerised by the pond, Reb scooped palmfuls of cool water onto the one leaf she could reach. She was fascinated by the liquid balls rolling down the green velvety contours.

I watched as she strained to reach a larger leaf when the inevitable happened, she overbalanced. Executing a silent nosedive, Reb momentarily disappeared. Cushioned by so many leaves, her graceful, slow-motion entrance into the shallow water struck me as hilarious. Reb begged to differ.

Spluttering, she clambered upright, water dripping everywhere.

'Sarong for you missy? Only five thousand rupiah. Sarong? You catch cold,' said concerned staff.

Her face creased. Tears were imminent. She felt mortified by the sudden attention. Waving the staff away, I dutifully intervened and asked for a towel.

Our meal postponed, we headed for the toilets where I removed her wet togs. But how to get her looking decent for the walk back?

I had a brainwave. My floor-length plastic raincoat in the becoming shade of gun metal grey, that I kept on hand for the many monsoonal downpours in Asiatic climes, would do it. Admittedly, it was too long but a la Tessa's influence, I folded it over at the waist and fashioned a cummerbund from a scarf supplied by a lovely Balinese lady – no payment necessary – to hold the lot in place.

Reb looked fine to me, but, unconvinced, she walked right up against me from behind in a Vaudevillian-style two step all the way back to our lodgings.

Having dropped Reb at her dad's for the day, I took a walk in the backstreets away from the tourist drags. I was shocked to find several cows grazing on what appeared to be a rubbish dump. One was methodically chewing the remains of an incredibly filthy plastic bag. I took a photo and was about to take another when a shrill, female voice demanded: 'What you do? Go 'way! You no b'long here. Go. Go!' and a tiny, middle-aged Balinese woman ran at me, flailing her arms. I didn't argue.

On another occasion we were befriended by a local woman and invited to lunch in her family compound which was an earth-en-walled affair comprising of open-sided sleeping huts for her age-ing parents and several enclosed rooms – presumably for living in, and two cooking areas – one outside, one in.

Seated on the floor, the centre of family attention, we were handed bowls of hot greasy water with chunks of pork fat floating in it.

'Drink. Drink,' she said.

I tried. So did Reb. But these were not flavours or textures we were accustomed to. Our host understood, seeming happy that we'd at least taken a couple of sips.

At the end of the meal I was asked if I could help their daughter, whom we'd not yet met.

'You are rich. You know things. You can help,' she said.

She then disappeared to fetch her daughter from a back room. The girl, aged about ten, appeared to have spina bifida. They obviously loved their child, wanting the best for her (don't all parents?) but they simply didn't have the resources.

I did my best to explain what I thought was wrong with her, but that it was beyond my ability to do much to help. They were very gracious of my let down and we made our goodbyes. Mmm. Troubles, even in paradise.

On a two-day, four-wheel-drive trip, with Reb, a new American pal and her hubby – again Reb's doing – plus a businesswoman from Oz, we'd stopped for the night at one of the many roadside, resort-style complexes.

As we were unloading our stuff from the jeep I noticed a sandwich board in the lobby of the hotel promoting the services of a skilled masseuse, his smiling face beaming healthily from the glossy photo attached. My Aussie companion and I booked ourselves in for the following afternoon.

At the appointed hour, modestly wrapped in sarongs, we were both looking forward to a relaxing massage. My companion went first.

A couple of minutes into the session I heard disgruntled, almost agonised yelps coming from the other side of the wall.

'Ow! Ow. Argh! Stop! STOP!'

Following an exasperated sigh, my red faced, dishevelled friend appeared.

'I don't know what's going on,' she said, 'But that's nothing like any massage I'm used to.'

As we'd paid up front, I decided to submit myself to the experience. I entered the room and proceeded to lie on the table thinking he doesn't look much like his photo.

I didn't enjoy my massage either. The penny dropped when we were walking back through the foyer. I read the advertisement again.

'What day is it?' I asked.

'Tuesday.'

'It says the masseuse is only available on Wednesdays.'

So who was that who'd just had his hands all over our bodies? It turned out, rather than miss our custom, the resort staff had multi-tasked. Our masseuse was the hotel gardener!

There was, in retrospect, a number of foolhardy things one could do in Bali. Attempting to travel as an independent female, with a child was up there. Almost every Balinese male I encountered asked, 'Where your husband?' as if to imply I was somehow incomplete or immoral not having a man beside me.

One silly idiot stood astride the front wheel of our parked motor scooter and refused to let go of the handlebars, even when I started it up. What he was trying to prove, I don't know. Perhaps he thought he was in with a chance – an Aussie woman and her daughter? Go figure. I didn't want to know and still don't.

Another daft idea was thinking I could learn to water ski in one afternoon. After several very painful faceplants, I gave up trying to stand from an unseemly squatting position and walked off. No reimbursement necessary. No more embarrassment, humiliation or pain either.

Scuba diving for almost eight year olds wasn't a hit either. If you haven't gathered by now I believed it important for my kiddiewink to experience as much as she could while she could. So I agreed to Reb's request to discover what Scuba diving was like – in the hotel pool. Anything to please the tourists! There we were – Reb, teeth and lips clamped firmly round the mouthpiece of the breathing gear, me wearing the oxygen tank, following diligently behind.

Starting innocently at the shallow end, it wasn't long before the floor of the pool descended and the water level rose from waist to chest height.

'Must be levelled out now,' I thought.

Another couple of steps and the floor sloped again. It was now level with my chin.

'Ah, Reb!' I called, giving the hose a tug.

Reb tugged back and kept swimming. I took one last step. This time the water went straight up my nose and into my eyes. I lunged forward, grasped Reb's ankle and pulled her sharply backwards. You should have seen the look I got. Stuff it. I pulled the plug.

Parasailing lost its appeal too. Strapped to the instructor, I went first and thoroughly enjoyed it. Then, while I waited on the beach, Reb took her turn. It wasn't until we were both back on terra firma that I learnt two tourists had been killed parasailing a couple of weeks earlier on this very beach. That was sobering.

Six months later, Reb also informed me that the guy who took her up put his hand down the front of her bikini bottoms. I asked why she hadn't said anything at the time.

'Because I was embarrassed and didn't want you to get cross,' she said.

Paradise's veil and our blinkers were definitely slipping, but I guess that's what happens when you travel – you become more worldly-wise.

Another daft thing we did was visit the temple monkeys. They were extremely agile, vicious, greedy little blighters who wouldn't take no for an answer. One climbed on top of my head and gripped my hair so tightly a welt was left on my scalp. Not wanting to risk being bitten if I tried to remove it, I walked around with the critter hat-like on my head until, 'Ow! Ow! Ow!' it decided to get off.

Again after the event, I discovered a fellow tourist had received a bite from one of the little blighters and needed a rabies shot. She showed me a nasty wound on her leg which was now healing, but it had suppurated for weeks.

Then there was the time we climbed an active volcano which we had to ourselves and our fifty-year-old guide who, to prove his fitness and show off, grabbed a flag pole marker and swung his body in a gradual arc until he was horizontal to the ground, and a stray dog that decided to follow us.

It was early and the morning mist gradually disappeared as we made our ascent. Along the route our guide produced panpipes and played a pretty tune. It's not everyday you're serenaded on a mountain surrounded by breath-taking vistas as dawn breaks.

Ninety minutes of climbing later I realised there was steam erupting from small cracks in the ground. That, and the soles of my sneakers were beginning to soften. F A R O U T!

I mentioned this to the guide. His smile did a disappearing act and turning-turkey, led us rapidly back the way we'd come.

Reb was entranced and envious of the a la Bo Derek hairdos that swung their brightly-beaded way through the day. There was a big smile when I suggested she might like her hair done similarly for her upcoming eighth birthday celebrations.

The next morning we'd made it to the main road, not quite one hundred metres away, before the first cluster of hair braiding ladies came into view. I'd hardly made eye contact, let alone negotiated terms, when they descended. There were at least eight of them, eagerly grabbing long tufts of Reb's blonde hair to vigorously ply their trade.

Her cries of discomfort at being set upon this way triggered my protective streak – I definitely had one, even if it seemed well hidden at times. I pushed my way past the many pairs of dexterous fingers to see her fringe, all six centimetres of it being deftly secured in tight minuscule plaits. Her face said it all.

'NO!' I exclaimed, loud enough for them all to hear. 'No fringe. No fringe.'

'Too late, Missy. We done already.'

'I don't care. I'm not paying. Not for the fringe.'

It registered. Her fringe was duly released from its torture. Poor Reb. In less than five minutes her entire head had been crowned with a myriad of braids. She looked great, but her pain threshold had been breached and we'd both been taken aback by the ferocity of the process. She courageously held onto her tears again. Forget anything to please the tourists. It really is all about the money, honey!

Encouraged by the success of our three-month trip I vowed to go somewhere interesting as often as I could from now on – preferably overseas. Reb, happy to go along – what choice did she have really – raised no objections.

So at the end of another's year work, teaching at the local college for me and the completion of grade three in primary school for Reb, we again took advantage of the generous Christmas holiday break granted by the education department and travelled to Chicago for six weeks to visit some friends. They lived in a three-storey brownstone, just like in the movies, with a shared entryway. We had to buzz to be let in. Our room was in the basement, directly below their street level apartment.

It took eight days of debilitating disorientation to get over the worst case of jet lag I've ever had. The windowless room we were in probably didn't help. Reb meanwhile, suffered no ill effects and was, by the time I emerged from my enforced hibernation, best buddies with my friend's two granddaughters. They'd all happily rollerblade together which was quite a challenge on the slushy snow-strewn Chicago streets, especially when they only had one pair of blades between the three of them.

Having re-joined the land of the living, I adopted the habit of walking the few hundred yards to the local drugstore each morning for a Chicago-style breakfast. This consisted of a half pint-sized coffee sold in an insulated plastic mug – my host had a cupboardful of the non-recyclable containers – and cinnamon or iced donuts, a baker's dozen (thirteen) to the box. Mmm…caffeine and carbs to kick-start the day from the drugstore. Now I understood why it was so named – bit slow I guess. In less than a week I was hooked.

One morning I noticed a guy standing out the front of the store. You couldn't miss him really. A black balaclava completely covered his head and there were no eyeholes that I could see. It was cold, but he couldn't be about to hold up the place – could he? I ignored him. He ignored me too, or so I thought, but as I passed his spot he emitted a high-pitched wail that raised the hairs on the back of my neck. Rattled, I shot through the store door, shutting it quickly.

'Are you okay?' the girl behind the counter asked.

'I think so but there's a guy outside with a balaclava pulled over his head making really weird noises.'

'Oh, him. He's harmless. He stands there quite often. He's homeless but never comes in for coffee, just brings his artwork to sell on the street.'

Another morning I was mulling over the contents of the food cupboard in my friend's apartment thinking cereal might be a more healthy and less emotionally upsetting alternative for obtaining sustenance in the mornings, when my friend commented over my shoulder, 'You know, there's likely to be more nutrition in the cardboard box than the contents.' I chose an apple.

There were more cautionary comments, these ones regarding the dangers of being in the wrong hood such as, 'You know, if you take a yellow cab to go sightseeing in the ghetto you might not come back. You'd most likely be gangbanged, beaten up and left. Don't do it,' she said.

Reb and I, despite clear directions, still managed to take the wrong route on our way to a local jeans outlet.

Within twenty minutes of leaving the apartment we'd become a couple of white honkies on the wrong side of the tracks. The paths and roads were covered in three inches of snow and hidden icy patches, and there was absolutely no one else about. No parked cars lined these streets. In fact there was very little traffic, and the buildings were a lot more modest than the ones we'd been among a block or so ago. Okay, it was a cold Sunday morning, which could account for the quiet, but this wasn't the place for us to be. I could sense it.

As we gingerly picked our way along the deserted, cheerless streets neither of us said a word, little clouds of exhaled breath accompanied us instead. In the unnerving silence, each window we passed became a question mark. Who might be watching and why? Every movement of the tree branches became a threat. Even a squirrel gave me the jitters when it scuttled by.

I attempted to break the eerie spell, 'This is ridiculous, Reb. No one's going to… Ow!'

A snowball hit the back of my head. I wheeled about to see a man across the street. He was pointing at us and calling something I couldn't make out. He stooped to gather more snow.

Not wanting any further interaction, I grabbed Reb's hand. 'C'mon. Let's go.'

I didn't know if the guy was harassing us, playing with us or helping redirect us. Regardless, the purchase of a pair of jeans was no longer part of my day's agenda, we – pardon the pun – legged it.

Another worrying event occurred when we were at home. My

friend's youngest daughter was in her bedroom practicing Wicca – as you do – and her two granddaughters, along with Reb, were tucked up safely in bed. I was curled up on the sofa reading and my friend was painting a whacky mural onto the top of a large dining table; a stylised tree of life in swirls of iridescent colour.

Around 8.30pm the buzzer to the apartment sounded. Not expecting visitors, my friend flipped on the intercom. It was one of her daughter's friends, so she buzzed him in. A teenaged boy around sixteen years old entered the room, his face was a sickly, pallid green. He said nothing, just walked on through, and I looked at my friend.

'What's wrong with him? He looks like he's going to throw up. Do you reckon it's drugs or booze or both?' I queried.

She said she wasn't sure but to give it a minute and she'd go and ask. She did and returned. 'We might be getting some more visitors very soon,' she stated. 'It seems our young friend was kicked out of home last night and in retaliation stole a CD, which he no longer has, from a music store, He dropped it on the street as he was running from some Puerto Rican store detectives. Those guys are hired because a lot of them are big and menacing.'

Sure enough, within a couple of minutes there was an horrendous hammering on the outer door of the apartment block and a voice the whole street could hear demanded if anyone was harbouring the young man observed running towards the building.

Since I was nearest the window my friend said, 'Take a peek through the curtain and tell me what you see.'

Heart clamouring, thoroughly unnerved by this sudden turn of events, I carefully moved the curtain a teensy bit away from the window. Three muscly, bouncer types were standing in the entryway. One had a red bandana on his head. I relayed my information.

My friend said, 'We're not under any legal requirement to let them in. They're paid by the store to stop thieves, that's all. They know he came in here. They'll probably contact the police. If they turn up I'll have to let them in but let me do the talking.'

I nodded, dumbfounded and apprehensive.

Fifteen minutes later the buzzer sounded again. This time,

credentials ascertained, my friend let three plain clothes cops into her home. All three had regulation buzzcuts, no necks, broad shoulders and wore custom-made business suits. They struck me as potential bully boys. One made a judgemental wisecrack about my friend's artwork.

'Into devil worship, are we?'

Suspicion confirmed. Wisely, she didn't take the bait but remained silent.

'We want to speak to your son,' he demanded.

'My son's not here,' my friend replied.

'Right. We want to speak to the young man who was seen entering this apartment.'

'Okay. Please come through to my daughter's room.'

Another of the detectives followed her while his cohorts remained with me in the lounge. They didn't speak and remained standing in the middle of the room. I was still curled up on the sofa reading, as if nothing untoward was happening. It was surreal.

After a couple of minutes the frightened, handcuffed teenager was frog-marched to the waiting squad car. The remaining keepers of the peace filed out, climbed aboard and the car pulled away. My friend clammed up. Not sure what to make of it all or her mood, I too kept my thoughts to myself.

No more was said about the incident that evening but I no longer felt safe. The self assured arrogance of the police and the imposing presence of the store's security staff definitely had an impact on me. All that muscle for one unhappy teenage boy acting out. What was going on here? Unsettled by what I had witnessed I did not enjoy the rest of the evening.

The next morning the young guy returned after spending the night in a police cell. My host, angered by his behaviour the previous evening, told him he'd jeopardised the safety of everyone in the house and as a result he was no longer welcome. She closed the door in his face. I was stunned by her action but refrained from comment.

The underbelly of life in Chicago was emerging. I'd already been told about 10pm curfews, whereby anyone underage on the streets after this time would spend the night in the cells. But this young guy, who'd run in panic over a $20 CD, now had a police record as well as nowhere to go. The wrong side of the tracks was simply too easy a place to find here. My interest in America took a nosedive.

Oblivious to such dynamics, Reb continued to rollerblade at every opportunity and at the end of our stay my friend's grand-daughter gave them to her. Thrilled, she came to tell me her good news, eyes sparkly bright.

'Can I take them home, Mum? Pleeeze!'

Difficult. Sending them by air would cost more than I was willing to pay, there was a risk they wouldn't arrive and there was definitely no space in our backpacks.

'You can, but you'll have to carry them. I suggest tying the laces together and hanging them around your neck.'

A couple of days later, Reb trudged her way through Sydney Airport, rollerblades swinging, happy as Larry. As for me, I'd never cried with relief returning to Australia before.

Chapter Nine

Back in the Land of Oz – Fire, Flood and a Build in the Bush

Despite being glad to be back in Oz, I had no intention of staying put – moving house regularly worked for me. Not so for Reb. On one house move I was awake at 7am, ready to commence loading the car and a one-tonner I'd hired for the day. As soon as Reb was up I fully expected her, now nine years old, to lend a hand.

Around 9.30am Reb appeared, yawning and still in her PJs.

'Can I watch telly?' she mumbled.

Although thinking the opposite I said, 'I suppose, but you know we're moving today.'

She nodded, stumbling towards the TV and an easy chair.

By 11am I was ready to drive the first load away. Reb was curled up, eyes glued to the screen, seemingly oblivious to the activity around her, a plate of leftovers and glass of milk on the floor beside her.

'Time to go, Reb. Are you coming or do you want to stay here?'

No prize for guessing her answer. Knowing she'd be safe enough – she always locked the door whenever I had to go out without her – I left with the first load, returning a couple of hours later. She hadn't moved and, despite a few requests for help from me, resolutely remained glued to her spot, eyes still focused on the screen. I was not concerned by her behaviour, just puzzled and wondered what was she playing at.

By 3pm, load number two was ready to rock'n'roll. Off I went, again alone. By 5pm the place was empty except for Reb on her chair and the TV, which she was still watching. I unplugged it and placed it in the truck. Only Reb on the comfy chair remained. She didn't move but sat cross legged on it watching me.

Light dawned. Fed up with moving house again, she had displayed one of the dastardly delights of passive-aggressive white-anting, the only way she could think of: making a stand, or, in her case, a sit.

I lifted her up, still seated on the chair, and carried her out on it. We were both laughing, but I'd finally really registered – Reb was not a mini-me tag along. I had my needs, and she had hers. For now though, I held most of the power so was doing what I could while I could.

Apart from travelling and moving house, another long-term itch was to build and live in a country cottage. However it wasn't until we helped some friends (Reb pulled her weight when she wanted to) relocate an ex-railway worker's cottage they'd bought for $6,000 – a cheap but effective home extension – that I realised what was potentially possible in country New South Wales.

I decided to sell my home in Sydney, and concluded the deal from a payphone on top of a grassy knoll in Tasmania where I just happened to be on holiday (Reb was visiting rellies in Adelaide).

Surrounded by a low-lying, wet and wild landscape miles from anywhere, I don't know whose idea it was to place a phone box there but it was inspired.

Feeding coins against the meter and straining to hear the action second-hand on the long-distance line, I could just make out the bidding for my house in the background. I had no idea what figure had been reached until my agent, aware that my coins would soon run out said, 'It's reached $230,000 and stalled, will that do?'

Considering I paid $64,000 for it, I said, 'Yes,' just as my phone money ran out and I promptly burst into adrenalin-fuelled tears. A wombat ambled by totally nonplussed. Good for him.

Happily, not only did I have enough funds to secure an investment property, there was sufficient change (with a bit of careful financial management) to construct a little cottage. Though first I needed to secure a block of land to build it on.

Since the capital available to me wasn't limitless, I carried out my own conveyancing on a house site which, despite a beautiful outlook across the valley, surrounding hills and a nearby creek – always a plus in Australia – no one else wanted. I believe this was due to a whopping great gumtree in the middle of it. But since I wasn't planning to build a large sprawling house the usual fears of falling tree limbs were irrelevant, so with no qualms I handed over the asking price of $11,000 and it was mine. Bargain!

Block secured, I drew up some floorplans and a friend's husband, Bob (yep, Bob) a licenced builder, translated my floorplans into blue prints which were suitable for architectural sign off.

The plans were then submitted to local council for approval. This took longer than expected because a neighbour complained about the prospect of losing her view, effectively of the toilet block beyond the tree, down the slope, over the creek and across the road on the camp draft site. Honestly, some people!

After a further $400 outlay, which was a week's wages, and another six weeks faffing about, during which time Bob climbed the tree and painted a corresponding roofline to my proposed dwelling on its trunk, it was agreed my cottage would be shifted one metre further back. Finally, everyone was happy and building work commenced.

This time Reb was as keen as I was, which was great. However, we couldn't remain in our current rental and achieve our goal, it was too expensive. We needed somewhere cheap to stay until our little place was built. We found somewhere. Boy, did we ever!

Friends of friends agreed I could have their place in the bush for minimal rent as long as I looked after (kept) their two pooches – Psycho, an ageing brindled mutt with one blue eye and one white, and a Cattle Dog cross we renamed Weazel Wooly Bear. That the house had no heating system, was not connected to the mains for power or water and the roof wasn't insulated was no deterrent. There was a generator in the shed, a header tank, gravity-fed cold water supply, the roof didn't leak and we liked the dogs. We moved in.

Our new abode had an uneven sand track leading to it and was nestled among one hundred and fifty acres of bush land. It was pretty isolated – our nearest neighbour was a good five minute hike away, then no one for two kilometres. Once on bitumen, it was a twenty minute drive to the town centre and civilisation. Other than that it was us, the dogs, a ramshackle house, and the flora and fauna.

Getting ready for work and school was the initial challenge of our recently adopted, very basic lifestyle. As the water would take too long to feed via the kitchen tap, the first one up in the morning – usually me – would fetch a couple of buckets of water from the header tank in the yard and put it in a large jam pan on the gas stove to warm up ready for use. So long as the gas cylinders didn't run out she was sweet.

The water took a while to heat, during which time we – swaddled in our PJs, two pairs of socks, slippers, mittens, scarves, beanies, jumpers, dressing gowns and sometimes even a blanket – ate a breakfast of toast and a boiled egg or cereal and fruit. It was cold in the mornings, even in summer.

By then the water, which dribbled through a canvas shower bag attached with string to the bathroom shower surround, would be hot enough to wash with. We got roughly sixty seconds of warm water each.

The winter months were something else. My boobs were blue with cold, our noses were bright red, and we'd jiggle about, our teeth audibly chattering. Our bodies were doing their utmost to warn us of the need for warmth.

However despite the harsh conditions, Reb and I remember those days fondly. Perhaps because living rough requires cooperation – the mother and daughter roles were replaced by equally vulnerable survivalists, friends even!

During the summer, while fossicking in the ferns out the back, I found a free-standing bath positioned on bricks over a small fire pit. You've got to be kidding me! All I kept thinking of were cannibalistic rituals and frogs cooking themselves to death in gradually heated water. We never did try it out.

Not long after we'd moved in, Psycho went off for her daily walk and didn't come back. A tick or snakebite perhaps, or simply old age? We didn't know but kept hoping for the best, initially searching for her morning and night. After a few weeks we resigned ourselves.

Wooly, the remaining six-year-old pooch, was a bit lost on her own but then Rastus, our neighbour's ten-month-old blue Cattle Dog pup, turned up.

It was the canine equivalent of courting an older woman. At midnight there'd be toy-boy scratching at the door, all pumped-up and ready for action. I'd let Wooly out and they'd tear off, love-biting and who knows what else? By dawn our gal was always fast asleep on the front porch, completely shagged as the saying goes.

We settled into our new lifestyle and quickly got used to the morning chorus of kookaburras waking us up instead of our alarm clock. We also discovered that we shared our patch with many critters, large and small. There were kangaroos, possums, echidnas, marsupial mice, frogs, geckos, lizards, galahs, sulphur-crested cockatoos, rainbow lorikeets, owls and wedge-tailed eagles to name a few. There was also a motley crew of spiders, mosquitoes, dragonflies, beetles, millipedes, ants, cockroaches, wasps, moths and the ever-present flies. A little bat even flew into Reb's bedroom in the attic of the cottage and stayed for a few days.

A more exhilarating brush with wildlife occurred one afternoon upon our return from town. Weary from work, I'd asked Reb to get out of the car and open and close the last of the three gates to our place, but instead of returning to ride on the bonnet for the last little bit, like she usually did, she decided to run on ahead while I parked the car.

Not really paying attention I snapped to as I reached our front entrance, which I left ajar on hot days in the vain hope of keeping the place a little bit cooler. There, with the end of its tail draped across the doorstep, was a majestic, solidly muscled monster of a carpet snake – and I mean HUGE – twelve feet long and eight inches round, quietly and confidently going about its business, effortlessly gliding on through our abode.

I shouted to Reb, 'Watch it. There's a snake!' as she yelled exactly the same thing to me from the backyard.

'What! Another one?' came her alarmed response.

'Where?' I shouted.

'Coming through the back door.'

Our living room was twelve feet across – that's how I knew how long it was. The snake, itself a little disconcerted by the arrival of two humans, made a quick but dignified exit and disappeared into the undergrowth. As for Wooly giving any warning, she was off in the bush herself, probably chasing kangaroos.

By this time our little cottage was beginning to take shape. By dedicating three days a week to being Bob's gofer and having him on-site four days a week, the two of us had certainly made headway. My jobs on the building site ranged from removing clay with my bare hands (there was insufficient space to use a shovel) from the bottom of all twenty post holes, helping with formwork, laying steel mesh, ferrying wheelbarrows full of concrete, and running errands into town – occasionally three times a day. The block was thirty kilometres from town and we only had access to a village shop which was handy for milk, but not building supplies.

My knowledge and experience of building trade tools took a huge leap when the slatted pine verandas and wooden flooring were laid. Already familiar with shovels, garden forks and pickaxes, it was time to get up close and personal with various saws, hammers, drills, screwdrivers, the spirit level, glue and nail guns, planes and sanders.

As it was now nearing summer, I took to wearing an enormous shade hat and virtually lived in shorts, t-shirts, work boots and the smallest pair of leather work gloves I could find – my hands aren't that big – and neither am I.

Arriving on-site by 9am, having dropped Reb at school on the way, I worked my little bottom off, helping to secure the uprights and cross members and staggering under the weight of support beams. As I didn't have the funds to hire more labour I simply had no option but to get on with it.

One morning I arrived to find Bob standing beside an enormous stack of light apple green, powder-coated window frames. Grinning, he turned to face me, pointed to the pile of windows and cheekily announced, 'Your first mistake.'

The frames did look very green stacked together. I'd thought matching the frames to the greenery surrounding our home would bring the outside in – a popular interior decorator's technique – making the place feel larger. At that point, I wasn't so sure of my choice but when the windows were finally in position they looked great. Bob apologised.

Work on the cottage continued at a steady pace while our everyday life meandered a bit. Firstly, isolation meant there were no longer any of the usual distractions of the surprising hustle and bustle of life in a country town, unless you discounted the omnipresent generator-powered TV that Reb loved.

Now ten years old, as soon as she came home from school and was loaded up with a snack (have I mentioned she loved food?) I'd ask, 'Have you done your homework?'

'Yep,' she'd say.

Or I'd say, 'Have you got homework?'

'No,' she'd reply.

The ritual formalities dispensed with, on went the telly. It wasn't until I noticed Cs regularly appearing on several of her school report cards that alarm bells sounded.

Reb had never been particularly academic, but the usual Bs, with an occasional A had been increasingly replaced with strings of Cs. I devised a strategy and told her that I could no longer tune the television in. In actual fact I'd disconnected the aerial.

Reb, never doubting my honesty, now had no option but to entertain herself. I kept my fingers crossed the ruse would work. Wouldn't you know, her very next report card evidenced the revised state of play. Straight As. The idiot box is well-named.

One morning while I was in my car I turned off the track that led to our bush retreat – as I'd taken to calling our temporary dwelling – onto the highway, and heard what sounded like a gunshot.

This was confirmed when something went zinging over my car's roof. Keeping low, just in case, I kept driving but decided to make a few enquiries. Apparently there'd been a long running feud between two local families – we're talking years – and every now and then a few pot-shots were taken, just in case anyone would be forgetting!

Next came the flood. I had been warned the creek running through the property occasionally flooded, but wasn't told that this could result in being cut-off from the access road. Then it rained – a continuous deluge of five days duration. The dry creek bed became a boggy marsh – ridiculously hazardous to drive through, slipping and sliding every which way – before ending up as a coursing current of malicious mayhem.

Instead of attempting to cross the stream in my car, I left it on the far side bank of the house and each morning Reb and I waded across. It also meant stripping completely, and with our clothes and a dry towel secure in plastic bags held above our heads, we negotiated the treacherous expanse between banks.

On the third day, already fed up with this newly instigated routine, which had to be repeated on the way back, I bought a second-hand, two-man Canadian canoe through the local trading post. It was ridiculously cumbersome but cheap.

Our first attempt at using it was hopeless. Even with a paddle each we had no experience of canoeing so my instructions were unsurprisingly ineffectual.

'Put your paddle in. No. No. The other side. The other side. Now make it like a rudder.'

'What's a rudder?' asked Reb.

No time for explanations. We were drifting aimlessly and in danger of being ferried along to a wider section of the creek with a much stronger current. Completing a couple of purposeless rotations, I finally gave up and clambered out (no easy task) and got wet all over again.

Having yet another think, I bought some marine twine, which doesn't rot in saltwater, from the local chandlery. I'd presumed the creek was freshwater but I wasn't taking any chances. I tied the twine around a tree on one side of the bank, waded through and secured it to a tree on the other. Then, sitting in the canoe, I guided its course through my hand, via the twine pulled by the current's flow. By this time the current was no longer strong enough to cause a disaster but the water was sufficiently deep to warrant the effort. We continued this routine for a fortnight, after which time the creek bed could be driven across safely once more.

Then there was the fire, which I'd noticed three nights previously as a sparse flickering glow on the back hills. I didn't realise the danger immediately – city slicker, remember.

On the second evening I rang a friend who was affiliated with the Country Fire Service (CFS) to ask if there'd been any reports. None.

Now more than a little concerned I rang the owner of the house to tell him I thought a fire was headed towards his property. He rang me back and said some of his mates would be coming out a bit later to create a firebreak.

Reassured, I went about my business. It got dark but no firebreak team arrived. Nine o'clock came and went. Still no one.

At 10pm four blokes in a beaten up truck arrived and began haphazardly clearing the grounds around the house.

After an hour I went to see how they were doing. My help as a female had not been required. However in the dark I tripped over something quite large and solid at the bottom of the back door step. One of the men was lying in the dirt, out to it. I smelt booze. Brilliant! My friend's house and our lives were in the hands of drunks. Too late now, a roaring blaze erupted along the cleared line and a mesmerising fifteen foot high wall of pulsating, eyeball searing flames enclosed our dwelling. I woke Reb to come and have a look.

She stumbled to the veranda, took one look, mumbled, 'Yeah. Fire,' gave me a withering look and shuffled back to bed. So much for sharing the excitement.

After about thirty minutes the flames died down and were eventually doused by the makeshift fire crew. They left around midnight after telling me what to expect when the bushfire actually reached us. We were duly instructed to stay put. Not knowing any different, we did. It was the right advice.

The fire hit at 4am. Again we were surrounded by a ferocious flank of flames. Though, thanks to the recently created firebreak, they were sufficiently far from the house and raced on, not bothering to devour our shelter or us. In hindsight we were very, very lucky.

The next morning the extent of the damage was more obvious. One of the owners' cars which was awaiting restoration, had been reduced to a burnt out husk, his top fence had turned into black cuttlefish splinters, the water pipe from the header tank had melted and one of the walls of the storage shed was charred.

This last was not the direct result of the bushfire, but the work of the boys sent out the night before. Better that than burnt bodies though.

We left for town that morning through a carbon black, eerily still, charred wasteland. Every so often smoking trees exploded as internal gasses ignited, shooting showers of jagged glowing embers from their charcoaled remains. Acrid, eucalyptus-scented, choking, grey smoke hung two feet off the ground, which meant I had to drive the car with the doors open and lean almost horizontal, steering with one hand while Reb observed the gravel, making sure I didn't veer off the track. It took nearly half an hour to travel the two kilometres to the main road.

From then things back at the cottage began to move quickly. With the kind help of a couple of friends, the roofing iron and all the insulation batts were firmly secured. Bob cheerfully informed me that a helicopter could land on my place – it wasn't going anywhere.

I took this to mean the house needed to be that stable and wondered about the wind factor out west. I definitely still had a lot to learn about life in the bush.

A couple of months before Christmas our new abode was almost ready to move into. The roof and cladding now complete, the oiling and varnishing of the internal timbers could commence, followed by painting and decorating. I did this myself too and was really pleased with the end result. It was a charming little wooden, pitch-roofed, single-storey, two-bedroomed, open-plan cottage, big enough for a single-parent family plus pets, in a relatively cute and quiet rural Aussie village.

Wildlife accepted our little place as part of the scenery. We hosted a resident huntsman spider about the size of my hand, which moved around the rooms in turn. It sat high in the corners of the walls and behind pictures. Occasionally protruding a hairy leg while I dusted, it was a definite heart starter. I actually didn't mind having it around. Though a major reservation was knowing we each eat at least three spiders in our sleep over a lifetime. I often entertained the mild heebie-jeebies of waking with long, thick, hairy spider legs drooping from my mouth.

A family of six yellow-tailed black cockatoos ascended routinely, searching for insects by systematically stripping the bark off young eucalypts that were growing next to the western facing veranda. I was tempted to reach out and touch them, but the thought of receiving a nasty bite prevented that. These birds were a lot bigger than they appeared in the sky and so were their beaks.

Kookaburras visited too. I fed one bits of bacon until I realised these birds, despite their laughing call, are murderous. One hot afternoon, I watched as one made short work of a hapless lizard that had been warming itself in the sun. I decided against encouraging them.

Three little mice (not blind) also dropped by. I was entranced by the antics of one that I'd interrupted in the pantry swinging by its tail, trapeze artist style, to reach for the shelf below. Quietly shutting the pantry door, I left her to it.

An enormous goanna (lizard), six feet at least, and powerfully built – I could easily make out its thick strong claws – startled me when it effortlessly moved into view. It was scaling the rivergum behind the cottage looking for birds' eggs. I'd been mindlessly gazing out the window while talking on the phone.

'F*** me!' I announced to whoever I was speaking to and hung up.

Then there were some more snakes. On one occasion, a green snake was innocently sunbaking on the veranda and hadn't sensed our presence (I'd just come in from work) when I opened the sliding door. A rapidly wriggling streak of green leapt off the deck, instantly camouflaging itself in the grass. We were about six feet up and until then I had no idea that snakes could jump. Apparently I'd given it the fright of its life. The proof? A three inch squirt of greeny-brown guck left behind on the timber. I felt rather sorry for it.

The next snake visitor was a little more worrying. Reb and I were sitting on my bed cutting out pretend dollar notes for her school art project when we both heard a couple of heavy clunks coming from the bathroom. Since we were by ourselves and the dogs usually barked if there was an unexpected visitor, we looked questioningly at each other.

'Wait here, Reb. I'll go and see what's going on.'

As quietly as I could I slid the bathroom door open a few inches. There, lying on the cool terracotta tiles, alongside our bath, was an aggressive, venomous, red-bellied black snake. Very gently I slid the door closed. I don't think it heard me, but the dogs had. They put in an appearance.

'No! I said, sternly.

Noting the tone of my voice they obeyed and backed off.

'What is it, Mum?' Reb called from the bedroom.

'It's a red bellied black snake. It's in the bathroom. It knocked the shampoo bottles off the edge of the bath. We'll have to keep the dogs away. They'll want to kill it but it will more than likely kill them. I'll call Wildlife Rescue Emergency Services (WIRES). In the meantime, I'll put some towels along the underside of the bathroom door in case it tries to come out.'

Once I'd secured the situation as best I could, I dialled the WIRES number and left a message. A guy returned my call about thirty minutes later. A further forty minutes and a trained snake handler arrived. He took one look and said, 'She's a beauty, isn't she? I think she could be pregnant, either that or she was looking for water. Whatever, it's unusual for them to come into someone's home.'

'Can you tell us how long you think she is?' I asked. I don't know why I have such a fascination with the length of things.

'Looks to be about five to six feet. Right. I'll get her in my sack and relocate her. It'll be some distance from here. You don't want her coming back, do you?'

With that he scooped her gently but skilfully into a purpose-made canvas bag using a long wooden handled hook and drove away.

Another afternoon, at a friend's house seventy kilometres from our place, there was an unexpected downpour of such ferocity its thrumming on the corrugated roof of her shed home drowned out any attempt to talk. We'd even given up yelling. Twenty minutes later all was still.

I took my leave, driving carefully along the gravel track so as not to slide into boggy ground. The sealed roads, once I reached them, were not just wet but covered in branches, twigs and leaves. It was more like the trail of destruction a wild wind would leave rather than rain. I drove about five kilometres further before being forced to steer around a tree lying across the road. By the time I reached the main intersection I'd negotiated several more. What had happened?

My thoughts turned to our place and Reb at home by herself. I tried calling on the mobile, it was out of range. Rounding the next bend I was forced to stop. The State Emergency Service (SES) guys were sawing through the trunk of an enormous eucalyptus that was straddling the road. They'd made one cut through and I realised they were removing a sufficiently wide section of the trunk to allow cars to pass until the whole tree could be cleared.

Back home nothing seemed awry. I found Reb indoors happily occupied. When I asked her if anything unusual had occurred she said, 'Yeah, about half an hour ago a bit of a wind blew up. Our washing got blown up the street but I found it all. And the mice got blown off the table.'

Reb kept two pet mice in a cage on the occasional table on the back veranda. 'They're all right but I've put a belt under the table and fastened it over the top of the cage in case it happens again. Why?'

I told her what had occurred at my friend's and the carnage I'd witnessed on my journey home – fallen trees, limbs and leaf litter everywhere.

The next day at school, Reb learnt that friends of ours – a single mum and her two children were taking shelter in their bathroom when the roof to their home was completely ripped off. Apparently a forty kilometre wide gale force wind had swept a swathe of destruction through the middle of town. My friend in the shed was at one end of it, Reb and I at the other. There was an incredible mess in between. We had been blessed again.

Chapter Ten

Bali Revisited, Bangkok and Chiang Mai

At the end of 1994, following the move into our cottage but before settling back into life's more humdrum routines, I took another year's leave without pay – one of the brilliant perks of being a teacher – and Reb and I left on our second grand tour. She was now almost eleven and I'd just turned forty-one. No qualms from Reb. She was keen to go and, as before, there was no resistance from the education department. I simply had to cover Reb's school year curriculum before we got back. I didn't envisage there being a problem and there wasn't.

Our first stop was Bali, where Reb got to see her dad again. She was excited yet philosophical about the prospect, for he would most likely be preoccupied with work. Reb made allowances for this eventuality and got busy herself, learning to gamble. I learnt, like many other places with a tourist mecca reputation to maintain, Bali wears a mask – an attractive one, but a mask all the same.

During our six-week stay, Reb and a duo of ten-year-old male charmers met almost daily for back-to-back siesta gambling sessions. Gathered around an outdoor coffee table, the trio good-naturedly accepted the foibles of Lady Luck, amassing or losing matchstick fortunes, oblivious to the array of exotic foliage and vivid blooms gently nudging their elbows.

I too was primed for a learning experience, which belied the soulful beauty of the place, via a comment from one of the resort guests who stated in passing, 'You can't always trust the locals.'

I didn't ask for clarification, actually forgetting his words until I hired a motor scooter and took a trip across the island, Reb riding pillion. Just about everyone waved as we tootled along the almost liquorice soft tarmacked roads, caught up in the feel-good factor of a glorious sun shiny day.

After four bum-numbing hours on the bike, we were hungry for lunch so pulled into one of the wayside resorts, glad of the shade and a chance to try some more delicious food.

An hour later, tummies full and thirsts quenched, we sauntered casually back to the scooter ready for a relaxed leisurely ride back to our homestay. That was the plan anyway.

'Hey, Mum, we've got a flat,' Reb observed.

What? There'd been nothing the matter with our tyres when we'd stopped. Could it have something to do with the heat? I took a closer look. No. Nothing to do with the heat, the rear tyre had been slashed.

Immediately I recalled my fellow guest's warning and realised what the flattened tyre was about – the tourists would have to stay at least one night in the resort. Ca-ching! Ca-ching! But the ploy back-fired (pun fully intended).

Typically proactive, I told Reb we were going to get the tyre repaired – though how I couldn't say. She didn't argue. I suspected she'd picked up on my irate mood and wisely kept her own counsel.

I demanded directions to the nearest garage. It was just over a kilometre away.

'Right. Let's go,' I said, all action and determination.

I handed Reb our daypack and my helmet. She wore hers. Then, no easy feat with a flat tyre, I pushed the motor scooter the whole distance, sweating, swearing and grunting profusely.

Thankfully, the garage mechanic and his family were a genuinely helpful, friendly lot, as most of the folk seemed to be when away from the tourist traps. Within twenty minutes, and for a total cost of $3, the scooter had a repaired and fully inflated rear tyre. No rip-offs here. I hugged and paid the man, and his entire family – parents, wife and kids – came to wave us off. We'd become minor celebrities.

Thirty minutes into our homeward journey an overcast sky delivered the expected afternoon downpour. The deluge didn't last a few minutes as was the norm. This one didn't let up for four hours, and neither did I.

Fearful of a repeat lunchtime experience, should we pull into another resort to take shelter, I kept going. Pelting rain stung my face and, since my helmet didn't have a visor, visibility was minimal. But I was on a mission and doggedly kept on going. Reb had no argument with my resolve. Her sense of fair play also trampled, she was behind me in every sense of the word.

Around 6.30pm, beyond drenched and completely shattered, we puttered back to the hire place, the carefree holiday mood we had enjoyed that morning long gone. All I wanted was to get us into some warm clothes, grab a bite to eat and go to sleep.

On our way to breakfast on another morning, Reb and I stopped to watch a women-only work gang trudge up steep winding slopes and down slippery ones with loads of Bali stone confidently balanced on their colourful headwraps.

Collected at 5am by the foreman for a 7.30am start, the women had been delivered on time for their nine-hour shift. There was no laziness evident – 'Bali time' seeming a ruse reserved for foreigners. Tonnes of rock needed to be moved, and it was hot. We watched as sweat in large soupy beads slipped from their resigned, shiny faces. I commiserated with them. Reb too.

Leaving the ladies to it, we carried on through the continuous rural sprawl, its canopy of lush vegetation housing brilliantly hued birds. One of the birds caught my attention with its pretty call. A delicate confection, it was swaying lightly on its perch, enjoying a gentle breeze – resting, watching, listening, gone.

Later that day, back in our room for our routine mid-afternoon snooze, a blaring radio broke my calm. I lay still and listened to the almost constant backdrop of noise to life in Bali – distant car horns, shouts, banging, sawing, drilling, a motorbike's relentless roar, then a truck's. Next a beetle battling above in the bamboo beams claimed my attention, as did grasshoppers scratching out their signature songs, a bandsaw, an unexpected cock crow, and the fun-filled shouts of children in the pool…was that Reb's voice?

Roused I called, 'Reb?' No response. I was definitely home alone. I got up to go and check on her whereabouts. Some life patterns never change.

Leaving our room, I walked to the edge of the gardens to observe the male workers secretly manoeuvring for a better vantage point from which to watch the foreign children at play. They stood or crouched as they pretended to prune, half hidden by the bushes and stared. I made my presence known and magically they were busy. Then, like the birds they too did a disappearing act.

Crops can't be grown in unnourished soil so occasionally a hint of manure – cow or chicken – drifted across our balcony from the paddy fields. There were three crops a year here planted by men, harvested by women, and tended by both. I felt privileged being privy to this glimpse of how other cultures manage their affairs and the underlying wisdoms that accompanied such.

I was also impressed by the number of artists, stonemasons, weavers, carpenters, bead workers, woodcarvers, and dancers and musicians I encountered. Many of these individuals were artisans by day and performers by night, occasionally enjoying a level of notoriety when touring Japan or Denmark as part of a government-backed performance troupe.

'Did you get paid a lot when you performed overseas?' I enquired once.

Wan smiled, 'No.'

Ah, okay. I get the picture.

Although I'd realised it before, another thing I thought about on this trip was how much unwelcome attention foreign women receive, particularly if there's insufficient evidence of a male presence.

A Balinese male's hand may swing round 'accidentally' to connect with a breast, even if quickly withdrawn. So out of keeping with what one's been led to expect, you wonder if that really did just happen. Foreign women are supposed to be out of bounds. Yet, as elsewhere, it's probably a case of 'don't try, don't get'. They catch us off guard.

Sometimes footloose and potentially insulting, Balinese gents will descend at the beach or a quiet resting point on the path.

'Hello. Where you from? Where you stay? Where your husband?' they enquire in that disarmingly charming, gentle manner they assume.

The friendly smile plays on the naïve trust of the laid-back female tourist intent on having a relaxing time. Intuition says, 'This guy's after something and it's not English lessons.'

It could be sex but it's more likely to be money. If he finds out where you're staying your cash could vanish along with your camera and anything else of value.

On a first trip, as it's so novel, no one minds spending on gold, silver, leather, clothing, cheap food and guided tours to all the scenic beauty spots such as Lovina, Candidasa, Nusa Dua, Dua Sanur, Singaraja and Tanah Lot.

By the second trip however, a change sets in. The quaint musty dustiness and visual poetry of timeworn cloth and artefacts no longer holds much magic. As I no longer wished to buy anything, I told all the street sellers who approached to go away (in Balinese words to that effect). It worked, but as Bali folk are busy making money for their cause – impressive ceremonies which command greater power and status for their family as well as the Gods' reward of continued prosperity – most tourists will remain remorselessly pursued by every street seller, bemo driver and tour guide.

Reb, who had spent a few days catching up with her dad via a couple of short – and – sweet solo visits (her dad kept long hours) and a farewell dinner that he threw in our honour, seemed content to continue our journey. She had long accepted that her dad lived and worked overseas and her parents, though no longer an item, respected each other. She also knew she was loved by both of them – no matter the circumstances. Time to move on.

Leaving Bali behind, we arrived in Bangkok around midnight on a typically claustrophobic, sweat-inducing Thai night.

Dressed identically in what had been crisp white cotton frocks, we were both looking a little wilted around the edges, but this was surely no reason for the bellhop who was assisting us with our luggage to give me a sinister sneer as we followed him into the hotel's lift. The unspoken code of the classier establishments, which I'd thought this was, didn't seem to apply to this employee. I definitely did not feel comfortable in his proximity. Perhaps he disapproved of our nocturnal arrival?

Thankfully other members of staff followed protocol, so over the next couple of days we relaxed and enjoyed the hotel's facilities. For some reason we had the expansive indoor pool all to ourselves, and there was a surprising and welcome level of peace as well as lovely food in the quaint restaurant with its huge potted palms and old fashioned ceiling fans rotating lazily overhead. Time out, finally.

Our respite however was short-lived as I'd scheduled only two days to take in the sights including the gold-domed palace, broken teacup mosaic work and organic sculptures. And then there were the omnipresent monks. Short of enlightened souls, my impression was of a bunch of males with schoolboy mentalities playing manipulative mind games. It was made clear they'd become unclean (heaven forbid) should a woman touch them. That didn't preclude them from leering at women or commenting about them between themselves, oh no. Short of treating them respectfully, I felt some of them would benefit from a good old fashioned slap.

Rather than take the train, we decided to fly to Chiang Mai in northern Thailand. Spiritual intervention perhaps? I later learnt that some months earlier three young male tourists, while travelling on the train to Chiang Mai, had been kidnapped and robbed, their Achilles heels sliced through and their heads bashed in.

I began – some might be thinking, finally – to question the wisdom of showing my daughter the world. The potential for exposing not only myself but Reb to danger while travelling the globe, hit home. But it was too late, we were here and needed to make the most of it.

During our six-week stay in Chiang Mai we were privy to an annual celebration ushering in the Thai New Year. Arriving completely ignorant of the proceedings we were bemused when, travelling in a tuk-tuk, someone threw a bucket of water at us. Soaked, we exchanged bewildered expressions. Our driver turned to us and announced, 'Songkran.'

'Songkran,' I repeated, mechanically. It meant nothing.

Arriving at our hostel I approached a fellow traveller and asked if he knew what it was all about. He explained that the Thais throw as much water as they can over an eight day period to ensure good luck and abundance in the year ahead.

The next day we ventured out fairly early, thinking we could probably dodge getting too wet with a bit of careful sidestepping. Impossible. We made it to the corner, a whole fifty metres, when WHOOSH a bucket of water caught me in the face. Then WHOOSH another bucketful saturated Reb.

'Gee, Reb. We're not going to get far at this rate.'

I was right. We attempted to make our way to a nearby cafe for breakfast. WHOOSH. Another dousing for both of us.

'Right,' I said, 'Forget the plans. This is war. We need buckets.'

I led Reb to the edge of Chiang Mai's city moat where people were lowering a variety of containers into the murky green water in readiness for more luck and abundance boosting.

Reb and I secured a couple of free buckets and were bending forward, side by side at the edge of the moat to fill them, when some stupid drucker pushed us from behind, headfirst into the warm lime slime.

The force of entry created an air pocket in my dress and pushed it in billowing folds over my head. Not only that, Reb completely disappeared from view under the surface of the water!

My thoughts went racing, 'Where's Reb? Can't see her. How deep's this flippin' moat? Is there anything else in the water apart from cholera?'

I couldn't see a thing. Not only did I have hair in my eyes, the water was completely green. Thankfully Reb emerged centimetres from my grasp. I grabbed her and attempted to control my still billowing, brown dress. Reb told me later that I looked like an enormous chocolate cupcake.

The numbskull who'd pushed us in stood grinning on the bank and holding out his hand to help.

'Happy Songkran!' he chortled.

'I'll give you Happy Songkran, you moron!' I yelled, short of punching him. 'My child could have drowned. I could have drowned. We both could have caught some horrible lurgy.'

His grin didn't waiver. He either had no idea what I was saying or didn't care, or he genuinely believed he'd done us the biggest favour by boosting our year's supply of good luck.

Absolutely sopping wet with filthy water streaming from the hems of our clothes, there was no point carrying on that day. As we travelled light, we'd need to get our clothes laundered asap.

We returned to the hostel to dry out, our wet clobber and personal documents soon festooning the little room. Thanks to the unexpected dousing, the ink in my passport had run, and all our travellers' cheques and paper money had melded together in my wallet. To speed up the drying process, I carefully peeled the cheques and paper money apart and put the whole lot in the dryer. The result was giant, crackly, crinkle-cut paper crisps.

Over the remainder of our stay, once Songkran was out of the way, we frequented JJ's, a bakery/restaurant owned and run by an American-accented Thai guy and his wife. It was here that I tried sticky rice with mangoes and almost choked when the gooey mass I'd eagerly shovelled in virtually vacuum sealed itself to the roof of my mouth.

Panicking I garbled, 'Web, ma mouf's gum'd up. Thith stuff'th's thik.' And using my fingers, not ladylike I know, prized the conglomeration from my upper palate, dribbling considerably over the tablecloth as I did so.

Wiping my mouth and fingers on a napkin I nodded to Reb, who was alarmed by my unmannerly antics, to indicate all was now well and continued eating my dessert with respectful restraint.

On another of our visits to JJ's, I asked a waitress what she earned each week. She told me it was around $45, with which she fed a family of eight. I told her I earned $45 per hour and barely got by looking after myself and my daughter. We were both astonished.

Our lack of knowledge of other cultures was further reinforced by an impromptu visit to the wet area of a food market. Wandering among the various aisles of fruit, vegetables and spices, we came to an abrupt halt beside a table of large enamel bowls containing what appeared to be huge chicken fillets.

'Wow! They're enormous. They can't be chicken, surely?' I was incredulous.

Not for long. The female vendor ducked behind the table, reappearing with a beautiful mottled frog about forty-five centimetres long. Securing the frog by its legs in one hand and holding a short wooden club in the other, with one deft movement she swung the hapless creature onto the slab in front of us and walloped it over the head. Stunned, its legs fell apart, exposing its underside.

A literally gut wrenching knife stroke followed as she spliced the frog down its middle. Holding the head in one hand and the organs in the other, she turned the frog inside out. Et voila – giant chicken fillets.

My ignorance of the slaughtering processes caught up with me. Reb didn't react favourably either. We both viewed frogs as beautiful creatures to be admired, not eaten. We took off, it was a bit too graphic for seven in the morning.

Another amazing thing we witnessed, while participating on the walk part of a three day walk, ride and raft experience, was the dinner preparations of a Thai Hill tribe woman.

Smiling for my camera, she wielded a small butcher's cleaver and efficiently produced a meal from two dead rats for her family of four. And, as one of the rats had been pregnant, she skewered four baby carcasses through the head and left them to smoke over the fire pit in the hut's floor.

I watched, absolutely fascinated as chop-chop-chop-chop-chop-chop, first one rat, then the other, was topped, tailed and relieved of its tiny clawed feet. A couple of neat cuts through the pelts from stem to stern and then the bodies, produced two fresh miniscule sides of meat. These were then duly pulverised by a series of rapid-fire strokes from the back of the butcher's blade. All the while the chef's grinning gaze never left my camera's lens.

Her actions produced a mince paste which she left for a minute, popping outside to return with a handful of straggly, thirsty-looking lemongrass. This too was finely chopped and added to the rat meat paste. She then rolled a small ball of paste in the palm of her hand and pressed it flat. Dinner preparations were now complete. One rat pattie and one roasted baby each for herself, hubby, son and daughter.

In addition to the rat pattie demonstration, we discovered a Thai/Cambodian style of sewage disposal – a hole in the bamboo floor of our living quarters, through which you excreted, to be gratefully received by pigs. No waste here. This was REAL survival.

The ride part of our three day trek was the most fun. Standing on custom built platforms, our troupe of travellers – the two of us, a young couple from Tasmania, a French woman and a chappie of indeterminate Asian ethnicity – climbed aboard our new pet pachyderms.

Perched behind each giant head, legs tucked in behind our respective elephant's enormous ears, we were soon seduced into an hypnotic reverie by their lolling gait. Every now and then one of our rides would produce a strident, foul-smelling fart which had Reb in stitches. It was gratifying to know she was definitely still enjoying herself.

On the rafting leg of our jungle experience, where we all got drenched again, I noticed deep blue hieroglyphic tattoos across the back of our guide when his shirt got wet. I was intrigued but didn't ask.

A couple of days later, as we waited in the airport for our plane to London, I was leafing through some glossy books and came across a photograph of a man similarly tattooed. Apparently they ensure good luck in business, so it's not uncommon for Armani suited Thai businessmen working in London, when not physically tattooed, to sport an undershirt decorated with the superstitious symbols of Thai tradition. Our culture offers spoken prayer, theirs is written. Vive la difference.

I also read in a paper – in a tiny column of five words by twenty lines – that the Thai Government had embarked on a campaign to relocate the Karen people from the hills to the plains. The government wanted the land. That the Karen wouldn't know how to survive on the plains – they were hill tribe people and would probably perish – didn't seem to be an issue.

I later learnt that many of the hill tribe people were not Thai, but Cambodian. After the Thai Government had succeeded in removing the majority of the Karen, they discovered they had lost a lucrative tourist attraction, so secured a token group of hill tribe people from over the border to replace them. Any remaining romantic reasons for lingering longer in Asia vanished. I was glad we were heading back to my parents' place in the United Kingdom.

Chapter Eleven

Ben Nevis, Big Breasts and Further Personal Tests

As Mum hadn't been well due to heart trouble, Dad came to Edinburgh on his own to meet us.

'There's Pop,' Reb exclaimed when he made his way into the arrivals hall.

Despite slower movement, a balding head and considerably more weight, Reb would recognise him anywhere.

'Hiya, Pop,' she called as she ran for a cuddle. It was familiar and loving all at once.

Dad's face lit up like it always did when he saw those he held dear. Despite his occasionally surly temper, he was a loving man.

Mum, when we arrived at the house two hours later, was equally as happy to see us – if less effusive. Mum's love, I now understood, was demonstrated through her neat and tidy home, and well made meals and gifts. We spent two happy weeks together.

At the end of the first fortnight, with Mum and Dad's Hawick home in the beautiful Scottish borders as our base, Reb and I embarked on a three week road trip of Scotland.

Despite an horrendous head cold and related reservations expressed by my mum about the wisdom of such a venture, I hired a Metro from Carlisle, fifty miles away. Before setting off, we filled the boot with a treasure trove of favourite childhood foodstuffs.

There were Mr Kipling's cakes (now readily available in Australia); French Fancies – petite sponge cubes covered in fondant icing; Jaffa Cakes – orange flavoured sponge-like biscuits dipped in dark chocolate; Oatcakes – a Scottish specialty which were not actually cakes at all, but hard, unseasoned oat biscuits; Rowntree Fruit Pastilles – chewy fruit gums, no longer in production, apparently; Bassett's Liquorice Allsorts; Walnut Whips – walnuts set on a biscuit base, encased in marshmallow, covered in chocolate, individually wrapped and considerably bigger than they are now; Snowballs – chocolate covered spheres of marshmallow dipped in coconut; and Wagon Wheels – two large chocolate-coated biscuits stuck together with jam.

There was *way* too much sugar I realise now but then, as with my childhood years, I didn't know any better. Recollections of my Cadbury Roses chocoholism caught up with me, but Mum had already plied us with those.

Youth hostel accommodation booked in advance, I established a daily routine of breakfast, three hours of driving (not necessarily in a straight line), and a leisurely ninety minute lunch break, wherever we happened to be when out would come the plastic plates, cups and cutlery, along with whatever we fancied from the boot. To keep things reasonably healthy, I also bought bread, fruit, vegetables, cheese and milk from supermarkets along the way.

Three hours later we arrived by the 4pm hostel book-in time popular in Scotland. After we'd looked around our lodgings, made up our beds and organised ourselves for the following day, it was time to make dinner in the communal kitchen. Any friendly chit chat with fellow guests usually led to playing cards, board games, ping pong or being entertained by someone playing a fiddle or guitar. We'd then toddle off to bed around 9pm for a good night's sleep, before more of the same the next day.

Our first port of call was Edinburgh, admittedly not a three hour drive from Hawick, but I went easy on our first day (I'm not a total Sergeant Major). We took a tour of Edinburgh Castle, walked through the grounds and checked out the historic displays. It was not of much interest to either of us, and although the Royal Mile-inspired souvenir hunt lit my torch, Reb I noticed, was marking time.

When I asked her what she'd like to do, she surprised me by enquiring, 'There's a Disney store somewhere here, isn't there?'

How she knew that I didn't know. She was, of course, correct. Now it was my turn to mark time – for over an hour – outside said Disney store while Reb did her own version of souvenir hunting. With funds bestowed by her loving grandparents, she bought a bright red plastic Mickey Mouse alarm clock.

That her choice of souvenirs wasn't traditionally Scottish would have disappointed my folks but we agreed to withhold that particular purchase from them.

We then drove into Glasgow and stayed for two nights. It was long enough to sense that it lacked the appeal of Edinburgh, despite its growing press as the cultural centre of Scotland. However it did give Reb the chance to go ice skating.

Reasoning that should I fall and break something and our trip would come to an abrupt end, I decided not to go on the ice. Reb didn't quibble. She got it. She could still be carefree, I couldn't. I resigned myself to waiting patiently once more while she enjoyed her Glaswegian skating session.

Fort William came next and the hostel which, according to the groundsman, boasted a ghost in our room. Exhausted from the day's efforts, we readily fell asleep but were unnerved by his story of a young woman who was imprisoned in the room for life by her father for falling pregnant to the gardener.

The tale was feasible; the Scots have been a violent, abusive lot. We also scared ourselves silly in one of the basement rooms when we were playing table tennis. Although the door, which kept slamming, may simply have been due to a draught, it didn't take long for Reb and I to convince ourselves that the place was haunted. After the third time it slammed we dropped everything and bolted.

The hostel at the base of Ben Nevis was our next stop.

Not intending to climb the highest peak in Great Britain, I did want to at least set foot on the track that took climbers to the summit. Dutifully I signed the book that lets the authorities know who's on the track and their time of departure. If there's no sign off signature within a reasonable number of hours, the hostel sends a runner – one of the mad but very fit young things who make it their business to literally run up the mountain and check against accidents. Unfortunately quite a few folk have fallen to their deaths.

So around 10am, after a lazy, almost solitary breakfast – there were only four diners left, Reb and I ambled along the path. As I had a cold and my nose was continuing to stream, forget tissues, I took along a toilet roll.

It was a beautifully clear sunny day and after we'd walked on the flat for about thirty minutes, I asked Reb, 'Do you want to go on?'

'Not really,' she said.

'Are you sure? It seems pretty easy and it's a nice day for a walk,' I said, brightly.

'Oh. Okay. Just a bit more then.'

We carried on for quite a distance, every so often stopping for me to blow my nose and to check if the other was tired yet. When I was Reb wasn't and vice versa. This technique got us to the halfway mark and our first snag – an above head height ridge right in front of us.

Somehow we'd wandered off the track, taking an unofficial shortcut across the face of Ben Nevis. Not wanting to retrace our steps, we decided to scale the six foot high obstacle. Using exposed bits of rock as handholds and with me to give her a hoist, Reb easily regained the path. Then it was my turn. Having struggled for at least three minutes – which on the side of any sized cliff face is an eternity – I heaved my leg onto the flat and, puffing from the exertion, dragged my body after it to lie flat on my stomach. As you may be aware, climbing's not my kind of thing at all. I sat up and blew my poor, sore nose again.

'Are you sure you want to go on, Mum?' Reb asked, anxiously.

'Yes,' I snapped. 'I've come this far, may as well.'

By then, when we turned round and looked back, the hostel was a pencil dot, way below us. We couldn't make out cars anymore and definitely couldn't see people. And it had grown much colder. Our lightweight, waterproof clothing, Reb's track shoes and my mum's fun fur-trimmed rubber gardening boots were flimsy protection for where we found ourselves. But the sun was still beckoningly bright in the sky. We were fine.

Another forty minutes and many blows of my raw nose later, the track petered out and the terrain was decidedly more rocky and snowy. A young couple, their three-year-old holding hands between them, overtook us. Reb and I were doing our best, we couldn't ask for more, so we continued on.

I mentioned to Reb that at the top there was a one kilometre wide snowfield. She was excited, that is until we reached it and she slid about a foot down the ice. Panicked, she promptly sank to her bottom and burst into tears.

'I don't want to go any further. It's scary,' she said.

As luck would have it, a man and two women came into view from the direction of the snowfield. Distracted from our potential dilemma, we watched them making their way towards us.

The man waved and said with a grin, 'Ladies, the summit's only forty minutes from here.'

We'd been climbing for close to four hours at that point. It was too long and too close to give up now.

'Did you hear that, Reb? Only forty minutes to go. I tell you what. Do you remember the certificates on the hall table in the hostel?' I asked, as I remembered that certificates stating you'd successfully climbed Ben Nevis were available for 50p.

She nodded.

'If you get to the top, I'll buy you one.'

She stopped crying, blew her nose, and, holding hands, we continued.

Crossing the snowfield wasn't easy. Biting, wintery cold air swirled around us and the icy terrain was truly tricky. You had to concentrate to keep your balance, the ice forcing shuffling baby steps, but as the gentleman said, forty minutes later we trudged onto the cement landing on the summit of Ben Nevis.

There wasn't much of a view – low cloud obscured most of it. It was a bit of an anti-climax, I thought, until another climber, an English guy, joined us and casually asked how long we'd been trying to get to the top.

'This is our first attempt.' I said.

'Is it? You lucky devils. I've been trying for five years and this is the first time I've made it. The weather changes so quickly here you never can be sure.'

I realised we'd been blessed yet again. I asked him if he would take our picture using his camera and send us a copy if I gave him some money for postage. I'd already used the last two shots on my film on the way up. He agreed, wrote down my address and then advised us to leave.

'You can get frostbite pretty quickly up here, plus the weather's starting to change. If a fog rolls in you won't be able to see very much, so I wouldn't hang about if I were you.'

I heeded his advice. We'd only been on the summit for fifteen minutes but my fingertips were tingling already.

The way down was as much work, possibly even more than the way up. Tired from the unexpected exertion of our successful ascent, our knees and upper thigh muscles felt every minor jolt on the descent. And as predicted, a light fog crept slowly around us, but by the time we got to the edge of the snowfield we were beneath it. At this point one of the fit mad young things ran by on his way to the summit, bounding from boulder to boulder. He wasn't even breathing heavily.

Further down we saw a young man and his two West Highland Terriers, presumably on their daily constitutional. He was throwing snowballs for his bamboozled dogs that couldn't figure out where the balls went, each disintegrating – the snowballs, not the dogs – on contact with the ground. The pooches kept going back for more. We kept going too.

Four hours later, exhausted and completely over it, we stumbled back onto the flat path, which led to the hostel. It was here Reb, knees wobbling like jelly (mine were, so hers had to be surely!) tripped and grazed her shin on a protruding piece of rock. Overtired she put on a bit of a performance, limping exaggeratedly for the remaining few metres back to civilisation. Her face lit up though when I bought her the coveted certificate.

Finally, at the end of our three week trip away, my outrageously rotten cold did a bunk and hasn't been seen since.

Our remaining week at Mum and Dad's was spent maximising our time together, my parents making sure to take some proudly posed Victorianesque family snaps before it was time for us to go.

Our goodbye, when it came, was still difficult because we never knew when it might be the last, for whatever reason. Dad even admitted he thought they'd made a mistake relocating to the United Kingdom upon his retirement. But they'd done what they'd thought was the right thing at the time. Don't we all?

There were no tears – it wasn't their way – just hugs, kisses and a heartfelt, 'God Bless.'

Following our six weeks in Scotland we stayed in Holland with Flora, Tessa's mum and Reb's unofficial grandma. One afternoon the three of us were browsing in a bookstore when Reb discovered *Rooie Oortjes.*

This iconic comic book publication was crammed with curvaceous (may as well be) naked females with in-your-face boob jobs, dummy-sized erect nipples and other titillating titbits – soft porn, essentially.

Reb was fascinated. I left her to it but when we were about to leave I asked if there was anything she'd like to purchase. She made straight for a copy of *Rooie Oortjes.*

Flora thought the choice a little odd for a ten-year-old girl, but was more amused than concerned. The language was a bit blue but Reb didn't understand Dutch and besides, as I later learnt, the language was not the fascination. Back at Flora's flat the comic disappeared into our suitcase. I promptly forgot about it and so did Reb. Just another travel souvenir, or so I thought.

Back in Oz several months later, Reb's room having reached 'tip' stage was in dire need of a tidy. Her technique for dealing with mess was to stuff her chest of drawers full, so I began sorting and folding the contents.

Expecting the large bottom drawer to be as packed as the others, I pulled hard and it opened in a rush. This was hardly surprising as it only contained screwed up balls of paper. Puzzled, I uncreased one of them to reveal a precisely drawn figure of a nude woman with pert breasts, a nicely rounded bottom and large Bambi eyes. Wow!

I unfolded another couple – more of the same. An unexpected and unusual stash, Reb had apparently traced the images then discarded them in the drawer.

'Reb, what's with the scrunched up drawings?' I asked. 'They're really good. Why did you screw them up?'

'I drew them but didn't know what to do with them,' she replied.

'You mean you traced over them?'

'No. I looked at them and drew them over and over until I could draw them by myself.'

The graphic designer in Reb was emerging, not sexual deviance. What a relief.

Following our week at Flora's we took off for Germany where, on the second morning of our stay in the youth hostel in Frankfurt, Reb returned from the kitchen asking excitedly if she could go with the young lady she'd been talking to.

'Mum,' she said seriously, 'You'll have to hurry up and say if I can 'cos they're leaving soon and I have to go tell her.'

'Hold up, Reb. Before I decide I need to at least meet this person.'

On that, Reb grabbed my hand and led me to the kitchen. A young woman in her early twenties approached.

'You must be Reb's mum. Did she tell you about our request?'

'Kind of. Something about being a mascot? Who are you exactly?'

The young lady revealed she was Captain of the English Women's Ice Hockey team, in Frankfurt to play an international final. Upon meeting Reb in the hostel kitchen, she and her teammates decided a cute and fun-loving little Aussie girl would make a great mascot for the day.

Reassured by further urging from Reb, I agreed to her going. But it wasn't until I was waving goodbye, as the coach pulled out of the car park, that I realised I didn't know the location of the ice rink. I had an anxious wait ahead of me. They weren't due back until 10pm. It was just 8am.

I could be forgiven for my oversight, I'd had other things on my mind – namely where we would be staying over the next three days. I'd not managed to book anywhere yet.

This thought at the forefront of my mind, I returned to our dorm. Sitting on the lower bunk was a new dorm mate. Eyes twinkling and smiling brightly, the well-built, healthy-looking woman announced vivaciously, '*Heilloow*. I'm Gabriella.'

'Hello,' I said, grinning back.

'I'm Rhea.'

We got talking like long lost friends about all the usual stuff – where we were from, our families and what we were doing in Frankfurt when Gabriella stated, 'I have a request to make. I hope you'll be okay with it.'

'Hmmm?' I intoned, intrigued. Gabriella was such an engaging soul.

'I've only been away from home a short time but I normally buy my kids a gift on trips away. As I've not had time to buy them anything, I was wondering if you and your daughter would like to come and stay in my home, as their present?'

I was genuinely surprised but heartened by Gabriella's suggestion. 'When?' I queried, thinking I'd need to modify our travel plans.

'Tomorrow. We could travel together and my husband will meet us at the station.

'How long for?'

'Three nights.'

'We'd love to!'

Apart from the friendly interlude with Gabriella, I spent the rest of the day worrying myself sick. What if something happened to Reb? What if she didn't return? What if there was an accident? What if…? What if…? What if…? She did come back. Bang on time. She'd had a brilliant day. Most of mine was shite.

The three of us left for Landau the following day. The train trip took several hours. When we arrived Gabriella phoned her hubby. She'd mentioned they only lived a couple of kilometres from the station. Twenty minutes later, however, we were still waiting.

I began to wonder at the time her husband was taking and said,

'Gabriella, excuse me, but if your husband's coming by car and your house is only two kilometres away why is he taking so long? Maybe something's happened?'

'Oh no,' she replied. 'We have a curfew. He probably hasn't left the house yet.'

'A curfew?'

'Yes. The government imposed traffic curfews a couple of years ago because of pollution levels. Only those in service industries are permitted to drive out of curfew. Everyone else has to stick to the time limits. We also have to drive at fuel efficient speeds to further reduce pollution.'

This was 1995. I was favourably impressed.

We had a great time at Gabby's. I just knew we would, especially when I spied a unicycle parked in the hallway and their ringing phone was finally located under a giant pile of clean washing.

Indeed, Reb loved Gabriella's children – Marieka, their teen-aged daughter and Tilman, their ten-year-old son (who developed a bit of a crush on Reb).

While I accompanied Gabriella on her part-time bus run for the physically and mentally impaired and to her friend's boutique where she was a part-time sales assistant, the three new chums frequented the local swimming pool during the few days of our stay.

On our third and final night we attended a local beer hall along with Herbert, Gabriella's hubby and enjoyed a performance by the Canadian group, *Harmonious Wail*. It was a brilliant end to what had been a jam-packed impromptu visit.

Following our stopover with Gabriella's family, Reb and I left for Munich and stayed with a couple we'd met in Bali. He was a politician, she a socialite. They had a beautiful ultra modern home, a gorgeous dog, an enormous toy bear which was bigger than Reb, a somewhat snobby daughter and thought nothing of paying $1,200 each for tickets to a masquerade ball. They were very kind to have us as guests but we weren't on the same page as with Gabriella and Co.

Then came Italy. Oh my. It was hot, smelly, and boring. I guess

I'm just not into naked statues and mosaics. Reb neither, for that matter. We gave it our best shot but our efforts weren't helped by our experiences there.

Upon our arrival in Rome, straight off the train, around 10pm, we were following other commuters through the railway underpass, tired and unsure of our bearings. I kept an eye on Reb who was just ahead of me in the crowd when, out of the corner of my eye, I saw the hand of a young man reach forward towards the zippered compartment on Reb's backpack.

Travelling in a foreign country can be a great cure for tiredness. Immediately alert, I announced loud enough for him and others to hear, 'Oi! No you don't!'

Flustered, he grabbed his accomplice's hand and off they took quick time through the throng. Welcome to Rome, Rhea, I thought, and immediately slid my bumbag to my front where I could keep an eye on it.

Later, during our two-week stay, Reb, Marnie (a fellow traveller from New York) and I went sightseeing, taking in the Colosseum along the way. Strolling casually through the stifling, fume-scented streets and chatting animatedly, the three of us were thoroughly enjoying our place in the world as international tourists.

After a couple of hours in the warm sun we turned back, taking a quieter route. A woman with two kiddies, one either side of her plus a bubby in her arms, meandered in our direction. She suddenly made straight for me holding out a large piece of cardboard with something written on it. The ink was faded so I couldn't make it out. As I tried to read the words, she pushed the board at right angles into my body just above waist level, obscuring my bumbag, which I'd worn to the front.

Something clicked in my head. Something about avoiding the backstreets. I raised a fist and brought it down hard on the cardboard.

'I know what you're doing,' I yelled, attempting to push Marnie and Reb out of harm's way.

Marnie jumped into the road and Reb rebounded off a lamp-post, jostling one of the children, who by this point, was tugging my camera strap on one side, while his brother had hold of my shoulder bag on the other. Too late, I was now in the middle of a tense tug of war but I wouldn't let go.

From the stream of expletives I received from the young woman, anyone would think it had been me that had attempted to rob her. I stepped out of her reach and two *strippen cartes* (Dutch tram tickets) that I'd left in my bumbag fluttered to the ground. The woman had skilfully unzipped it and helped herself whilst I'd been distracted by the children.

'They didn't jump out all by themselves, did they?' I demanded, angrily.

Realising the jig was up, the woman gathered her kids and made off, still swearing and gesticulating.

Marcie asked me if I'd lost any money, but still shaken from the shock of the attack I wasn't sure. She kindly guided me to a coffee shop and helped me check the contents of my bumbag. The thief had snaffled a couple of hundred dollars worth of travellers' cheques but without my passport they were worthless.

Next we tried our luck at the Vatican, but the queue was so long that when we finally got in it was totally anticlimactic. In addition to being stuffed to bursting with tourists, it was fresco on the ceiling overkill and we soon grew tired of walking around looking up.

And I'm not sure what occurred on the Ponte Vecchio in Florence, but something decidedly creepy. While we were walking over the bridge, a hunched, cloaked, cowl-hooded character ambled towards us, rather like the old crones in fairy stories.

As we passed each other, fierce, black, energy-crackling eyes in a weather-beaten, slack-skinned face momentarily blazed up at me. Surprised, I looked away but distrusting my initial observation turned to see where the monk had gone, for that's what common sense was telling me this 'being' was. But he/she/it had vanished. Really weird.

Then, towards the end of our time in Rome, I became ill. I couldn't breathe properly; it was probably due to the pollution. Having had a total gutful of the place, I pinned a picture I'd drawn of a pizza to the YHA noticeboard. The pizza was covered in all sorts of junk: crushed cans, broken furniture, litter and piles of steaming poo, surrounded by seven arrows, all leading OUT of Rome. Guess the artist in me was needing expression.

Finally, on the afternoon of our departure, unaware that we'd been under anyone's scrutiny, Reb and I joined the regular troupe of backpackers waiting quietly for the bus to the city. It was another laid-back sunny day and there was nothing untoward, that was until a severely sweaty, middle-aged woman wearing large, dangly earrings and an ornate summer frock caught my attention.

Walking with two men in identical heavy denim blue jeans and black t-shirts, she seemed out of place among the fresh faced shorts and t-shirt backpacking throng.

A bus, already pretty full, pulled up and we all squeezed in. I suggested to Reb that she sit next to a man reading his paper, while I remained standing next to her in the aisle.

As more people got on however, I was progressively jostled towards the rear of the bus. In addition, I became aware that the two jean-clad henchmen were crowding me. One placed his hand partially over mine as I held onto the upright steel support, so I slid my hand a smidge or two further down the pole. His hand followed, violating my personal space. It was also surprisingly intimidating.

Uncomfortable, I let go of the support completely, wishing to remove myself from their proximity but found I couldn't. I'd been deliberately sandwiched between the two of them and in the crush in the back of the bus there was no room to manoeuvre. I stayed calm and caught Reb's eye over my shoulder. Thankfully Reb had been vigilantly scrutinising my movements.

I mouthed, 'Watch out,' and inclined my head towards the woman stealthily making her way through the overcrowded bus. The two of us watched as she slipped her hand into a number of passengers' bags. Totally over her behaviour by the time she stood next to Reb, I snapped.

'Stop the bus!' I commanded. 'There's a gang of pickpockets

on it. Him! Him! And Her!' I said as I inclined my head in their respective directions.

'Yep,' came a voice in agreement. It was one of the other passengers. 'She's had a go in my bag.'

'And mine.'

'And mine,' echoed two others.

The bus driver pulled over. The three thieves, taking their time about it, traipsed off. But as the bus pulled away from the kerb the driver inexplicably opened the middle doors as we passed the woman, now standing outside on the kerb.

Rearing her head back and suddenly jerking forward, hands on her hips, she viciously hawked a huge gob of spit straight in my face.

'EWWW!' everyone groaned in unison as I stood there, dripping.

I hadn't thought at the time that the bus driver may have been in on it – makes sense though. He could have been the husband and father, he certainly looked old enough. We live and learn.

The arrow we followed out of Rome led us to Greece, though getting there was yet another challenge.

First we had to get to Brindisi in southern Italy. This included a 'free to backpacker' overnight stay on the deck of a ferry. Romantic for some, but it was horribly cold spending a night under the stars. Notice I didn't say anything about sleeping under them. Although I managed a bit of shuteye, Reb didn't get any. Tossed around by huge swells, loosely covered with a jacket and other rolled-up clothes serving as a pillow, she hated the entire experience. Strike one against Greece in her book.

Arriving at the station in Brindisi in plenty of time for our train connection, I stowed our luggage in the racks provided, thinking our bags would be automatically loaded onto the train. This reasoning was either delayed airport mentality, my very first senior moment, or plain and simple stupidity – take your pick. In addition, too much waiting around on the platform resulted in doubt creeping in regarding the reliability of the train schedules.

Checking with an equally-fazed couple of travellers resulted in the four of us, though no one else from the throng (was that a clue?)

boarding the wrong train. One stop along, the young man in our group stated, 'We're going the wrong way. We have to get out and get back. If we don't there isn't another train until tomorrow.'

As soon as the train pulled up at the next stop, luckily just a few minutes later, the four of us jumped off and ran back along the tracks. Admittedly it was a bit dangerous, but we didn't know the roads so it was the most direct route.

With no previous long-distance running experience plus daypacks on our backs, we had about twenty minutes to cover a kilometre in searing heat. It was definitely a shake-up we could have done without.

We eventually made it to Athens, but my luggage didn't. It was where I'd left it, though the penny still hadn't dropped. Confused and distressed when told my luggage was not on the train, I was asked a series of rapid-fire questions by railway staff and eventually heard, 'Come back later.'

I did – twice that afternoon and a third time the following day, just after lunch. Feeling decidedly unkempt, sweaty and on the verge of tears, the stress of long-distance travel beginning to make itself felt, our bags, tightly trussed together with string, were finally handed over. I was extraordinarily relieved and extremely grateful.

I unexpectedly felt quite at home in Athens for it reminded me somehow of Sydney. Then I realised why. A lot of Sydney's suburbs and architecture – the low-lying two to three-storey buildings and wide pavements – were influenced by the Greek population there. It was inner city Sydney all over.

Reb did not feel the same way. Initially drawn by the smell of the open air yiros stand near our hostel, the garlic and yoghurt she had on hers for dinner, along with the exhaust fumes from heavy traffic proved too much – that or the meat was off. Whatever, Reb suddenly bent over double, clutching her stomach.

'Going to be sick?' I enquired.

She nodded.

'In the gutter, quick.'

She made it just in time, throwing up violently.

Embarrassed, as I knew she would be, I reassured her that it was okay. The street cleaners would deal with the mess, no one would mind. Though being off her food was considered sacrilegious to Reb (a Chinese Year of the Pig) and definitely strike two against Greece.

Reb also took umbrage to the 'I don't give a rat's' Sydney attitude of the locals. Especially when a souvenir toy she'd dropped on the bus was sucked along the floor by the air flowing through and whisked out the open door at the front.

In the passengers' defence it happened quickly, but that no one attempted to reach out a foot or hand to halt it on its way was strike three and you're out. Reb's face said it all. She was done. Time for us to go elsewhere.

To cheer her up, I booked a day trip to the island of Kea. The blue water ferry ride from Athens was very relaxing and so was the island. We sauntered along, checked out the various street stalls and bought a couple of souvenirs. Then we had something to eat, no vomiting this time, before meandering through a couple of backstreets towards the beach. Reb went straight into the sea (mucking about in water another of her favourite pastimes), while I sat quietly on the sand observing. Around 4pm we headed back to the ferry, carefree holidaymakers once again.

A week after our arrival in Greece we used our Eurail passes and travelled onto Paris. Wishing to dispose of some rubbish when we arrived, I located a bin at the station. Unexpectedly, it had a two centimetre thick, steel plated lid bolted to it.

'That's strange,' I thought. Undeterred, I looked for another. It too had a metal lid. 'What's with the steel lids?' I wondered.

I became aware of a public address message every few minutes warning passengers not to leave their luggage unattended as it would be taken away and disposed of. A bit over the top, I thought, as were the *gendarmes* walking around in threes.

Initially I thought such behaviour on behalf of the French judiciary must be customary in Paris. That was, until in frustration at not finding any unlidded bins, I asked another commuter where I could find one. She said I probably wouldn't as they had all been sealed shut following a recent bomb attack at a station, which killed fourteen people.

Now the PA warnings and trios of *gendarmes* made sense. And as we would be sitting around in the station for the next two hours, I reasoned that if it was our turn to go, there wasn't much I could do about it, so I stopped worrying.

The two hours passed without mishap, we boarded our train and headed for the south of France with the rubbish stuffed in the top of my backpack. It could wait.

We enjoyed our stay in the south of France, visiting Saint-Tropez, Saint-Raphael, Cassis, Nice and Monte Carlo.

The genteel old-world carousels, giant wooden crab sculpture on one of the clean and crunchy beaches; bright, white, bottle-blonde, suntanned, beach-babes; luscious chocolate shops and a bona fide artist straight out of the 1920s in his white Panama hat, shirt, slacks, espadrilles and sweater slung casually around his shoulders as he went about his work, were all so typically French – ooo la la.

Lulled into a false sense of confidence, I tried out some of my incredibly rusty high school French in a bakery, asking stridently for, '*Un cochon rouge,*' and pointing at a pink fondant mouse.

The poor saleswoman looked baffled.

I repeated myself, a little louder. '*Un cochon rouge, s'il vous plaît.*'

'Madame?' She raised an eyebrow and also pointed at the mouse asking, '*Cela?*'

'*Oui,*' I replied.

'*C'est une souris rose, madame.*'

She was, of course, quite correct. I hadn't asked for a pink mouse; I'd asked for a red pig.

Another memorable gaffe of sorts occurred when the European equivalent of Japan's bullet train, the TGV, hurtled out of nowhere at a phenomenal speed, rocking Cassis' aged railway station where Reb and I had been calmly sitting eating lunch and soaking up the ambience.

All of a sudden our hair and clothing were engaged in a futile struggle with forces beyond their control. Thankfully, Reb had the presence of mind to clamp her hand down on my straw hat to prevent it from being blown away, but our food wasn't so lucky. Four seconds later, peace resumed and you'd be none the wiser.

'Holy Moly, Mum. That was scary.' Reb exclaimed.

I agreed.

Sitting at a railway station at an unscheduled stop, I now realised, was not a good idea. We continued on our way.

After France, it was on to Spain and Portugal. I found the extended afternoon siestas in Barcelona from 2pm until 5pm, when nothing was open, extremely frustrating. So did Reb.

With nothing much to do in the afternoons, we did what we could in the mornings, visiting the Olympic Stadium and the Tibidabo Amusement Park which is on top of a mountain. Then, following our stopover in Madrid, where we checked out Gaudi's house, I decided to cut our Spanish stay short.

Wandering around looking at tourist attractions wasn't working for us. We just weren't Spain's kind of culture vultures. No hard feelings, we dropped in on her poorer sister, Portugal, and after only two days visit returned to France.

Back in France we stayed in Marseille where, while washing our clothes in a laundromat, we met a young woman struggling to remove her double bed duvet from a dryer. We went to her assistance, got talking and she appointed herself our personal tour guide over the next few days until we left, once more, for Paris.

The hostel we stayed in Paris was one of the trendiest yet. It had a bar with a dance floor, lots of mirrors, strobe lighting, comfortable chrome and leather seats around coffee tables, as well as a small restaurant and communal kitchens. It was a pleasant change from the bare bone basics of most of the other hostels we'd stayed in.

I took Reb to the Eiffel Tower. On my first visit, aged twenty-one, I'd been chased up by three young Italian guys. This time I posed beneath it with my daughter, and fifteen years later I posed beneath it again, alone, to mark life's stages (and to show off a little).

Around 6pm, as I was disinclined to do any more that day, a young Australian policewoman who was staying in our dorm took

Reb to see the lights of the Champs-Élysées. The plan was (here we go again!) for them to return around 7.30pm by Metro – Paris' underground rail system.

Come 10pm I was pacing up and down the street outside, the accelerated ageing process striking again. We were due to leave the next day and Reb needed to be back, in bed and all to be right with my world. A further thirty minutes and there they were walking briskly towards me, chatting amiably.

'I'm SO sorry we're late,' Ms Law apologised, explaining, 'There was a bit of a to-do. Another bomb scare. It was probably a hoax but all the trains were stopped and we had to get off and wait on the platform until the all clear was given. The trains started running again about half an hour ago.'

'I was a bit worried, but these things happen,' I said. 'I'm just glad you're both back. Thanks for looking after Reb.'

On that we shook hands and called it a night.

The next day Reb and I returned to Holland, staying at Flora's to start with, before arranging a further three months stay with another friend – a professional violinist and freelance photographer.

Our new host was hardly in the place, which was great, as we were free to come and go pretty much as we pleased. Plus we received a couple of bonus invitations to attend concerts at the Royal Concertgebouw, where he was performing.

Initially impressed, I soon realised that it would be easy for seasoned classical musos, who have learnt the scores by heart, to no longer notice the finery and fripperies, the sweeping staircases, candelabras, marble sculptures or the gilded stucco of grand concert halls as it's become second nature, to the point of boredom.

They leave home at the last minute for their evening shift, puff on a cigarette in the alley before signing in at the backdoor of the theatre, pull on their stale, grubby, penguin suits and march to their places to perform, as per that night's conductor. Upon conclusion, the obligatory bows and smile of acknowledgement are carried out by said conductor to an appreciatively clapping and respectful audience.

Behind the scenes, there's no friendly camaraderie but rather snide comments from intellectually bored and creatively frustrated, cliquey people with a job to do caught on the treadmill as much as any of us. I was chagrined by this state of affairs, but it's understandable.

Despite such disillusionment, I took the opportunity to investigate potential residency and citizenship in Holland. Not so easy. Holland's once famous open-door policy is now pretty much a thing of the past. I would need forty hours of work a week – two more than the workload for a married man. The logic being, since I was a single parent, more money was required. In addition, I'd need proof of a place to stay and a guarantor for at least five years.

To start the ball rolling, I had my credentials translated into Dutch and started looking for work. I was initially offered two hours teaching business protocol to German, Swiss and Dutch bankers but realised, very quickly, that forty hours of work like this a week would leave very little time for a life, let alone the need to look after Reb. Plus, there wasn't much of a window granted to fulfil the conditions. If they weren't fulfilled, I could face deportation to try again in another six months.

Ever the optimist, I enrolled Reb in an international school. The school absorbed the lion's share of my funds, but I was just happy that Reb loved it.

At 8.45am, cheerily lit against the wintery fog, the white three-storeyed school building on the side of a canal looked like a Dutch-themed gingerbread house. Reb's young woman-of-the-world persona felt right at home with the friendly caring staff and twenty-five different nationalities in a class of twenty-six students.

Each day she received only an hour's lesson in English, other than that it was Dutch all the way. But I'd never known her so willing to leave her bed in the mornings. We were getting up at 5.45am in the dark to catch the train and two trams to get there on time and not one word of complaint from Reb. AMAZING!

The requirements for residency however, eventually proved too difficult and my initial buoyant hopes of remaining in Holland fluttered to the ground and stayed there. Sensing my disappointment, my host did his best to cheer me up and invited me along to a couple of his photographic assignments while Reb stayed with Flora.

The first one was in London at the Barbican where, in the middle of a rehearsal led by Sir Simon Rattle, my friend's mobile phone (which he'd left in my care so he could take photos from the balcony) rang. I wasn't sure what to do – switch it off, answer it or take it out.

I opted for the latter, though not before Sir Simon who looked over his pedestal with baton in hand declared, 'Oh, don't be embarrassed.'

I'm not sure if he was being sincere or sarcastic but it made no difference, I was scarlet to my toes.

Complete with press pass, I also made an appearance as my friend's assistant photographer at an erotica exhibition – a highly creative display of all things erotic, including semi-clad male and female models parading body-paint designs on their toned torsos, or sporting seriously sexy lingerie and bondage outfits. There were also vases with vagina-shaped orifices, sensual handbags of leather and fur, even an enormous chandelier of inflated and illuminated condoms, if memory serves me correctly.

Some of the models were also part of elaborate table decorations. One remained immobile for two hours, covered in luscious fruit and greenery, unexpectedly striking a different pose once sufficient food had been consumed from around her reclining body. Her movement provoked gasps of wondrous surprise as none of the gallery-goers had thought she was real.

Another model in a similarly lengthy back-breaking pose stepped away from a three-dimensional promotional display to strut her stuff on behalf of the promoters. More wow factor. I totally enjoyed myself and even remembered to take photos.

I was also introduced to a sculptor of cement sheep (which made sporadic appearances at roundabouts), some experimental musicians and had my hair cut and styled by a professional hairdresser and body painter.

Life can be a lot of fun in Holland, but this was it for us. Time to return to Australia, though not before a brief detour to the United States, well Walnut Springs in San Francisco to be precise.

We stayed with a 'Keep In Touch' family a mutual friend in Australia had shared with me. 'Keep In Touch' folk were happy to host overseas travellers (helping to cut their accommodation costs), as well as provide the means for meeting new people.

Dave, who was over sixty years of age and the head of this particular 'Keep In Touch' family, worked three jobs each week. I wondered aloud how he managed to keep going. He revealed it was a matter of necessity.

'My nine-year-old son was kept in a coma, on life-support, for a year before we decided to let him go. The bill was $500,000 and if it's not paid back, the hospital will take the house in lieu. So, while I can, I'm paying what I can.'

I was gobsmacked. That this kind of thing could happen was a relatively new concept to me.

Then there was an incident at the shopping centre roundabout when a young male passenger in a passing car proceeded to take pot-shots out of the window as the vehicle made its way round. Dave and his two daughters automatically bent over and ran for cover.

Reb and I, momentarily stunned, followed suit. 'What was all that about?' I enquired from behind the safety of a parked car.

'Who knows, Rhea? This kind of thing happens quite a lot and sometimes the idiots use live ammo, so no point taking any chances,' Dave replied.

I was gobsmacked again.

We spent one week with Dave's family before heading to Hawaii, our last US stopover before Australia. With only a few days to enjoy it, I wasted no time hiring a car. At one point we'd stopped at the lights of a four-way intersection. A Hummer pulled up on the road to our right, its wheels the same height as our roofline. It waited, audibly thrumming, it was a big vehicle.

On the front passenger seat was a massive Rottweiler. I hadn't paid much attention to the driver until Reb's voice piped up, 'WOW! BIG CAR! BIG DOG! And little him.' She grinned at me from ear to ear. Reb's insinuating comment about this chap's ego was spot on. I hadn't laughed like that in quite a while, it was a memorable marker to the final stage of our second world trip together.

Chapter Twelve

Back in the Land of Oz – The End of the Road

Soon after we returned to Australia Reb turned twelve and our lives took on a mainstream tone for I knew, based on what I'd experienced, that it was best to remain put while she completed high school.

So, our days of gallivanting curtailed, we set about selecting an appropriate school for Reb's needs, making appointments and interviewing the heads of several, before formally applying.

Despite not being religious, Reb gained acceptance into a Roman Catholic school. We believed it was the best the region had to offer, so felt honoured and chuffed.

As the school had a reputation to maintain and strong principles to uphold, wearing a school uniform was mandatory (demerit points were freely issued for non-compliance) and included a dress with box pleats, which had to be adjusted for each student.

Confident my high school sewing skills would suffice and not wishing to fork out for a professional seamstress, I assured Reb that I'd manage the hem of her new dress by the time she'd be needing to wear it. The pleats wouldn't be an issue. This was on the Friday before school started. I had the whole weekend. Piece of cake.

Come Monday, all I'd managed to do was look at the tacked pleats in complete bewilderment before deciding to snip the tacking thread. 'That's not right,' I thought as the pleats billowed out from their confinement.

'Reb, I'm sorry but you'll have to wear your dress as is until I can find time to fix it. I'm sure it'll be alright.'

Reb left for school in her new school uniform. That her dress wasn't finished was blatantly obvious. The skirt was now a billowing diamond shape. It stuck out from the waist, angled in at mid-thigh and followed a tapered slope to her calves, rather like a giant Chinese lantern, except this was grotesquely cumbersome and she was wearing it.

That afternoon when I fetched Reb from the bus she emerged not in her dress but in a pair of grey winter shorts.

'Where's your dress?' I asked. 'I thought you were supposed to wear your summer uniform?'

'I am. I had to get special permission.' Pregnant pause. 'It was granted. No questions asked. The dress is in my backpack.' This statement was accompanied by an indignant, 'Stop-faffing-about-and-do-the-right-thing' look.

I took her and the hapless dress straight to JJ's, the local tailor. No further quibbles from me about the cost; I didn't dare.

Despite this initial faux pas on my behalf, Reb loved her new school and quickly became a key member of a close-knit group of friends. Her school life taking shape, she still had to survive life at home, for it was one thing to be on the move with her mum but quite another to lead a more mundane lifestyle – as we were both finding out.

Another morning, Reb left for school to discover – courtesy of the bus driver and an otherwise empty bus – that there was no school that day. She'd overlooked the notification. As a result she came home at 2pm instead of 5pm. A latchkey child, Reb often returned to an empty house, indeed she expected it.

My being home this particular day was unusual. I'd finally taken advantage of flexible working hours, and knowing the side gate was secure, had double-locked the front door, turned the music up and was going about my business, semi-naked (it was hot) oblivious to the outside world.

Initially unconcerned by muffled noises from outside – we lived next door to a second-hand furniture shop so there was always some noise or another – I carried on 'til I heard a thin yodelling wail.

'Mu-uuu-uuu-uuu-mmm!'

That's Reb. Confused, I rushed out the back and around to the side double-gates. Reb, ridiculously, was suspended from one of them. She'd obviously tried to clamber over it but as she'd jumped down, the leg of her voluminous skorts (a cross between a skirt and shorts) had slipped neatly over the rounded top, halting her progress a frustrating ten centimetres from the ground via an enormous wedgie. Realising this was not the time to fall about screaming with laugher – see, I had learnt something about mother-daughter relations – I said, 'Hiya, Reb, what are you doing back from school so early?'

'Why didn't you answer the door?' she asked.

I detected a marked, petulant tone.

'I didn't hear you.'

'Well, I knocked AND rang the bell,' she said, accusingly.

'I didn't hear you, Reb.'

Reb was now a well-built young lady and she most certainly didn't look comfortable.

'Would you like me to get you something to stand on?' I enquired.

Before I got an answer there was an almighty rip as the last of the stitches in the crotch of Reb's skorts gave way. The garment parted company, right through the middle. This didn't help her much though as the elastic waistband wasn't affected so she was still attached to the gate.

I'm sorry folks, but at that point I lost it completely and doubled-up in laughter, tears trickling down my cheeks. Even Reb saw the funny side and managed a wan smile.

'Oh, Reb, I'm sorry. I'll get you down.'

A further five minutes later, and Reb regained her freedom and sunny demeanour. The skorts were in halves. I suggested we take them to JJ's. The tailors were doing quite well out of us.

Uniform issues all sorted, Reb was happy, initially, to travel the one hundred and twenty kilometre distance each way, every day, to her new school and back. After about a year however I suggested she might like to board through the week rather than commute daily, returning to our cottage on weekends. This would give her more time in the evenings to complete her homework, plus she'd feel less travel-weary. Reb seemed relieved, but as we had no relatives nearby to potentially come to the rescue, who would she stay with?

I asked for assistance from the college and Reb started boarding with a family near the school, an arrangement which lasted six months, during which time her capacity for independence blossomed. When she was living with me she got up forty minutes earlier to press her pleated skirt. She knew better than to wait for me to do it. Me do ironing? I'd stopped ironing when I'd left home and I wasn't about to go back there again!

Reb then stayed with some good friends of mine a short bus ride from the school for a further six months, before landing a longer-term arrangement in the home of another friend.

At the age of fourteen she had her own room, was responsible for making her own meals, washing her clothes, keeping her room in order, getting up and going to school on time, and completing her homework. She seemed to manage all of this effortlessly on an allowance I could afford, which wasn't much, and I remember being impressed by the hospital corners on any bed she made. However there was an emotional glitch that I'd definitely not seen coming.

One afternoon Reb arrived home for the weekend, let herself into the house – she now had her own key – and found me sitting on the couch, watching telly with our pet pooch, Stumpy (a dachshund). Suddenly she announced in a heart-breaking wail, 'You love that dog more than you love me,' and burst into wracking sobs.

I had absolutely no idea what had precipitated such an outburst. When she'd left for school that Monday she'd seemed her usual sunny self.

Dumbfounded, I moved over on the couch so she could sit down and put my arms around her while she sobbed her heart out.

When she'd cried herself out, I offered tissues and a glass of water and asked her if she could tell me what had upset her. It transpired that a number of her school friends, taking advantage of Reb's natural affinity for listening and wise counsel, were offloading their worries and woes onto her. Not knowing how to deal with it all she'd become overwhelmed. Apparently this had been going on for the better part of the year.

I suggested that I speak with the school's counsellor to ask if he would meet with her and reveal some strategies she could use to protect herself in the future. She agreed. So that's what happened.

Normal transmission was resumed and the next couple of years flew by, me occupied with my role as a part-time educational facilitator and part-time parent, and Reb in her role as a full-time, semi-independent student and part-time daughter. Without fully realising it, we were gradually working our way free of each other – such is life.

Then, aged sixteen years, Reb was selected by Rotary to live in America for a year as an exchange student which accentuated further the life processes already in motion. Selected on her own merit to be an ambassador for Australia, she was thrilled to be leaving.

My daughter was a force to be reckoned with. She didn't need her mum much anymore, but I realised how much I'd needed her along the way. Life can be cruel, can't it?

Upon her return to Australia, Reb spent a further two years at home, still boarding through the week until, successfully completing her matriculation, she was accepted into a graphic design course in South Australia and moved interstate.

Gone.

Reb was gone.

There was now a yawning chasm, which I had no idea how to fill. My little girl was growing up, gravitating gracefully and naturally towards her own way to go, and I was left to continue mine once more.